DATE DUE

JAN 27 1992			
OCT 11 1993			
DEC 29 1993			
AUG 29 1995			

DEMCO 38-297

The American Destiny

Volume 15

The Darkening Horizon

The Darkening Horizon

The American Destiny

*An Illustrated
Bicentennial History
of the United States*

*Editor in Chief
Henry Steele Commager*

*Editors
Marcus Cunliffe
Maldwyn A. Jones
Edward Horton*

The Danbury Press

EDITOR IN CHIEF: Henry Steele Commager has taught history at Columbia, Cambridge, Oxford, and other universities, and at Amherst College, for over forty years. He is the coauthor (with S. E. Morison) of *The Growth of the American Republic,* and author of *Theodore Parker, The American Mind, Majority Rule and Minority Rights,* and many other books. He is the editor of *Documents of American History* and, with Richard B. Morris, of the fifty-volume *New American Nation Series.* Professor Commager was recently awarded the Gold Medal of the American Academy of Arts and Letters for his historical writings.

SENIOR EDITORS: Marcus Cunliffe is Professor of American Studies at the University of Sussex. He has been a Commonwealth Fellow at Yale and has taught at Harvard and other American universities. Professor Cunliffe's books include *The Literature of the United States, The Nation Takes Shape, Soldiers and Civilians,* and *The American Presidency.*
Maldwyn A. Jones is Commonwealth Fund Professor of American History at the University of London. He has been a visiting professor at Harvard and at the universities of Chicago and Pennsylvania. Professor Jones has written extensively on American ethnic groups and is the author of *American Immigration,* a volume in the *Chicago History of American Civilization.*

Library of Congress Catalog Card No: 73-8423
© 1976 Grolier Enterprises Inc
Printed in USA
ISBN-0-7172-8113-2

The Danbury Press
A Division of Grolier Enterprises Inc
PUBLISHER: Robert B. Clarke
EDITORIAL DIRECTOR: Wallace S. Murray
ADVISORY EDITORS: Edward Humphrey, Bernard S. Cayne, John S. Cox, Alan H. Smith, Hallberg Hallmundsson, Donald R. Young, Robert L. Hurtgen, Eric E. Akerman, Frank H. Senyk

Orbis Publishing Ltd
EDITORIAL DIRECTORS: Martin Heller, Brian Innes
MANAGING EDITOR: Edward Horton
DEPUTY EDITOR: Sam Elder
ART EDITOR: Derek Copsey
PICTURE EDITOR: Lynda Poley

Contributors to this volume include:
H. C. Allen, University of East Anglia; Raymond A. Esthus, Tulane University; Robert H. Ferrell, Naval War College, Newport, Rhode Island; Manfred Jonas, Union College, Schenectady; Nancy Greene Jonas, Veeder School; Armin Rappaport, University of California, San Diego; Bryce Wood, specialist writer on Latin America.

Introduction

Twenty-three years elapsed between the end of hostilities in the First World War and the Japanese attack on Pearl Harbor that brought the United States into the Second World War. Throughout that period the American people remained hostile to the kind of internationalism Woodrow Wilson had preached and were unwilling to enter into binding commitments of the sort that membership of the League of Nations entailed.

Despite the rejection of the Treaty of Versailles the United States did not retreat into what Wilson called "selfish and sullen isolation" or turn its back completely on the outside world. The Republican administrations of the 1920s pursued an active, though independent, role in world affairs. Indeed, through such gestures as calling the Washington conference of 1921–22 and the signing of the Kellogg-Briand Pact of 1928, the United States took the lead in the search for disarmament and peace. At the same time she sought to promote the economic stabilization of Europe by tackling the thorny questions of reparations and war debts. There was even some collaboration with the League of Nations on non-political matters. But that there were limits beyond which Americans were not prepared to go was shown by the Manchurian crisis—the first link in the chain of events that was to lead to the Second World War. American public opinion condemned Japanese aggression, but it was even more opposed to any action which might lead to war.

However limited the role of the United States in Europe and the Far East there could be no doubting her intense concern for the Western Hemisphere and especially for Latin America. But the inter-war years saw a gradual retreat from the "big stick" diplomacy followed by Theodore Roosevelt, Taft, and Wilson. American forces were withdrawn from the Caribbean protectorates that guarded the approaches to the Panama Canal and in 1934 Franklin D. Roosevelt formally repudiated intervention. The Good Neighbor policy, as it was known, did not wholly dispel fears of Yankee imperialism in Latin America, but it softened animosities and paved the way for an era of hemispheric friendship.

From the beginning of the 1930s it was evident that the uneasy peace established at Versailles was breaking down. Japan's Manchurian adventure was swiftly followed by the rise of totalitarianism in Europe. Tension mounted as Hitler sought step-by-step to reverse the Versailles settlement and as Italy's Mussolini echoed his menaces. By 1935, when Germany remilitarized the Rhineland and Italy invaded Ethiopia, it was clear that Europe was heading for another war. In the United States isolationism and pacifism were now at high tide. They culminated in the passage of the Neutrality Acts of 1935–37, which were designed to ensure that America would not be drawn into a European war in the way that had happened in 1917.

Japan's renewed attempt to conquer China in 1937 and Hitler's rape of Austria and Czechoslovakia convinced Roosevelt of the folly of isolationism. He favored collective action to preserve peace. But his hands were tied by the continued opposition of American public opinion to international commitments. The outbreak of war in September 1939 did not greatly affect American views about the wisdom of neutrality, but the success of the German *blitzkrieg* in the spring of 1940 had a stunning effect and led to a major change in American foreign policy. After the fall of France only Britain stood between Nazi Germany and the domination of western Europe. Meanwhile in Tokyo an expansionist government had come to power, dedicated to the achievement of Japanese hegemony in eastern Asia. Thus the United States suddenly faced the prospect of finding itself hemmed in and friendless in a world dominated by two aggressive totalitarian powers. Roosevelt, concluding that a Nazi victory would endanger American security, abandoned neutrality in favor of a policy of aid to Britain by all means short of war. The Lend-Lease Act of March 1941 formally ratified that commitment.

By the summer of 1941 the United States was not only the "arsenal of democracy" but was waging a naval war against Germany. Hitler would have been fully justified in declaring war upon her. But he did not. War came to the United States from the Pacific, not the Atlantic. It resulted from the hard line Roosevelt took toward the Japanese. He was not willing to allow Japan to expand into Asia and denied her the supplies she needed to wage her war in China. In effect therefore Japan had to choose between abandoning expansion or striking a blow at the United States. She chose the latter.

Contents

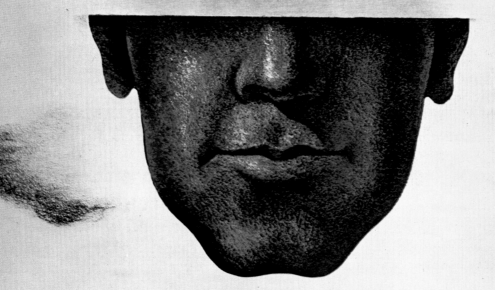

"business as usual"

AMERICA
open your eyes !

Chapter I

THE COLLAPSE OF WORLD ORDER

Ever since Washington's time, the United States had had a profound dislike of foreign entanglements, and after 1918 the disillusion with war reinforced the overwhelming desire to concentrate on domestic, rather than foreign, affairs. Yet many people refused to turn their backs on the outside world. The antiwar mood fostered a burgeoning peace movement and influenced the Kellogg-Briand Pact which aimed at ending all war. Successive administrations took part in conferences to limit naval armaments and secure payment of the vast war debts owed to America. But by the early 1930s, the naval limits had been flouted, Europe had defaulted on its debts, and each nation grappled in its own way with the problems of depression. Postwar hopes for a new order based on cooperation and trust had evaporated.

Retreat from Internationalism

If ever there was a time when the peace of the world might have been ensured, and was not, it was the 1920s. The years between the Paris Peace Conference and the Great Depression saw the failure of American foreign policy—and, to be sure, the policies of other nations. The world, as a result, can only regret the loss of the simplicities, the wonderful possibilities, of an era that has slipped far into the past.

And yet, looking closely at the 1920s, there is great difficulty in seeing just where statesmen might have done better, for the period was not friendly to the large visions and bold acts that were necessary to protect the future. The American nation found itself in an unaccustomed position. Its intervention in the European war had helped make that huge conflict a world war. Intervention

had assured the victory of the Allies. But the people of the United States had never before taken any sustained part in the balance of power in Europe, and it was only natural that after the war they would withdraw their influence to such locales as the Caribbean and Central America. That was not all. They failed to understand the management of their own economy; they did not sense the increasing interconnectedness of world trade and finance; nor did they comprehend the damage that a single individual such as Hitler could do to the fabric of civilization. For all these

reasons, the opportunity for peace after 1918 was lost.

The American retreat from internationalism after the victory of 1918, which is now seen as a grave historical error, became clear with the presidential contest of 1920 between two small-town Ohio newspapermen, Warren G. Harding from Marion and James M. Cox from Dayton. Their backgrounds reflected the local interests of the American people, their willingness to put aside the aspirations of what was becoming known as Wilsonian idealism, and to return to the ruts in which foreign policy had run for decades.

The ailing Woodrow Wilson tried to make the election a solemn referendum over the League of Nations, but from the beginning it was an uneven contest and soon turned hopeless. Governor Cox fought a fairly brave fight. In many ways he was an able man. He knew that the league issue was a millstone around his neck, and this knowledge did not make him entirely convincing to the voters. He was not "sold" on the league until he and his running mate, Franklin D. Roosevelt, the wartime assistant secretary of the navy and distant cousin of the Republican Roosevelt, visited the White House after their nomination. There they saw Wilson sitting in his wheelchair, managing a wan smile, insisting that the light shone ahead upon the path to the league and nowhere else, as he told the Senate a year earlier in July 1919. After talking with him, Cox dictated a strong statement supporting the league. It would seem that the two nominees were shocked at what they had just seen, that the spectacle of the invalid rather than any serious process of logic had moved them to this commitment. During the campaign they sometimes lessened the obligations the United States might assume if it entered the league.

Senator Harding was careful not to lose any votes during the campaign. The Republican candidate did not travel around the country, on the advice of Senator Boies Penrose of Pennsylvania who told party managers, "Keep Warren at home. . . . If he goes out on a tour, somebody's sure to ask him questions, and Warren's just the sort of damn fool that'll try to answer them." Harding's front porch was enlarged, and from there he delivered short, inane speeches which he privately called "bloviations." The election was never in doubt, and Harding won in November by a landslide.

After the electoral verdict there was some hope that Harding might undergo a conversion to internationalism, but the hope eventually was dashed. To the interested individuals who called at Harding's home, the president-elect confided only opaque glimpses of his policies. The conversations were full of jollying and cordiality, and

Woodrow Wilson left office bitterly disappointed at the Senate's rejection of American participation in the League of Nations. The ailing president is shown here chairing his last cabinet meeting.

During the 1920 presidential campaign, the successful Republican candidate, Warren G. Harding (shown at left making one of his "front porch" speeches), had adopted an ambiguous attitude toward membership of the league. In his inaugural address he stated emphatically: "We seek no part in directing the destinies of the world." The Democratic team of James M. Cox and Franklin D. Roosevelt (below) endorsed Wilson's commitment to the world body. But they were roundly defeated at the polls.

(contrary to the law) were often accompanied by bourbon and scotch served by the "Duchess," as Mrs Harding was known. Problems of the future did not often arise. The president-elect did not seem to favor the League of Nations as it had been established in Geneva, but he still looked to some kind of association of nations. During the campaign it had been said that, in imitation of the principles of his predecessor, Harding had taken fourteen positions on the league. After the election he sought to combine them into a favorable reference or two in his inaugural address, but according to one story, Mrs Harding blue-penciled them during her revisions of the text.

The new Harding administration also formally ended the war. America had never ratified the Versailles Treaty which contained the covenant of the League of Nations and so was still formally in a state of hostilities in 1920. Harding therefore authorized a separate peace, the Treaty of Berlin, which omitted those sections of the Versailles Treaty dealing with the league or supporting any league-directed activities connected with the making of peace. It refused for the United States any territorial indemnities or obligations in the form of mandates, and awarded only sufficient reparations to pay for the small army of occupation which remained in the Rhineland until January 1923.

America thus witnessed the triumph of nationalism over internationalism in 1920–21. Many people wanted nothing so much as a return to the life they had known and enjoyed before the war. "The boys"—2 million of them—had visited a France that was hardly in a position to show its best face, and they did not like what they saw. There was probably no greater single influence in moving American policy away from internationalism than the disillusionment of the soldiers, which had spread throughout the United States by the time the election of 1920 was held.

In the middle of the year a collapse of wartime prices had begun to throw the country into a recession that lasted well into 1921. The war was obviously responsible. In the entire history of the United States government until April 6, 1917, $24 billion had been spent out of the federal Treasury. But in the following eighteen months the nation spent an equal amount, not counting $10 billion lent to the Allies during and immediately after the war. The sudden flooding of these funds into the economy swelled prices beyond reason. Farmers entered upon a period of bad times that would last for twenty years; the prosperity of the later 1920s failed to touch many of them. Among city folk caught by the postwar recession were two young Kansas City haberdashers who had met in the army—Eddie Jacobson and Harry S. Truman. They found themselves with an oversupply of expensive shirts and neckties, and there was nothing to do but sell out at a loss. Jacobson went bankrupt. Truman managed to make precarious arrangements with his creditors, but for years thereafter was plagued by debts.

The bad times of 1920–21 vastly helped to discredit internationalism, and to lead to a resurgence of nationalism. The immediate desire was to move affairs back to the years prior to 1914. The New York *Sun* had predicted that when the war came to an end a lot of people would pick up their 1913–14 thoughts right where they had laid them down. The feeling of disillusion was overwhelming. According to the Milwaukee socialist Victor Berger, all the war had done for America was to bring flu and prohibition. Harding said that the United States needed "sustainment in triumphant nationality" rather than "submergence in internationality." Author and editor George Nathan remarked with majestic indifference: "If . . . half of Russia were to starve to death the day after [tomorrow], it would not matter to me in the least. . . . For all I care the rest of the world may go to hell at today's sunset."

Opposition to the World Court

Despite the decisiveness of the Democratic defeat in 1920, there were many, many Americans who continued to look wistfully toward cooperation with the peoples of other nations. For a while these individuals, for the most part residents of the Eastern Seaboard and of large cities of the Middle West and West, sought to interest their countrymen in a substitute for the League of Nations.

The league unfortunately had not been within the tradition of American foreign relations. Article Ten of the covenant had contained a principle almost directly contrary to previous American ideas of proper organization of a world community. Under this article, members of the league undertook to respect and preserve against external aggression each other's "territorial integrity and existing political independence." Woodrow Wilson's disclaimers notwithstanding, Article Ten looked in the direction of military force. American traditional thinking had connected peace not with power but with orderly process. Americans had concentrated on arbitration and conciliation and international law. This was the tradition of the *Alabama* claims arbitration against Great Britain (arising from the construction of Confederate vessels in Britain), the arrangement of bilateral treaties for arbitration and conciliation, and the codification of international law on such occasions as the Hague Conferences of 1899 and 1907. If only President Wilson had drawn the covenant along these lines rather than as a virtual guarantee of the territorial status quo. Whatever demon had possessed him in his sudden decision—it was sudden indeed, as he made up his mind about the nature of the covenant only in late January and early February 1919—it persuaded him to take the wrong turning. The error was sensed with great clarity by both his supporters and his enemies. It is hardly an accident then, that one of the president's leading critics, Elihu Root, was the virtual father of the "protocol" or treaty establishing the World Court, which Root and a group of international jurists drew up at The Hague in the summer of 1920.

The World Court was within the American tradition of internationalism, and Root fully expected it to receive the support of Congress. But he did not count on the obstructive nationalism of leading Republican senators who happened to be outright enemies of Wilson's ideas and hence of anything even remotely connected with the league. They seized upon the fact that the World Court was authorized to give advisory opinions to the league's

An agricultural recession followed the First World War and buttressed the desire to tackle domestic, rather than world, problems. Thomas Hart Benton's painting shows a farming couple in the lean 1920s.

Senator William E. Borah was a leading (and eloquent) opponent of American membership of the World Court.

In his vociferous campaign against the court, Hiram Johnson stressed the primacy of national interests.

Elihu Root helped draft the protocol for the World Court and urged acceptance by the United States.

council. Therein they saw danger to the very foundation of the Republic.

The World Court fight is worth attention in detail, because it showed the forces that could be arrayed against even the most modest, not to say inoffensive, proposals for cooperation with the political activities of the League of Nations. Senator William E. Borah of Idaho was adamant in opposition to the World Court. This immensely talented but essentially negative statesman was very powerful. Borah had been in the Senate since 1907 and in his first years had taken interest mostly in domestic matters where he displayed a Progressive temper and voted for any measure that might benefit his state. During the war his interest turned to foreign affairs, and he proved the most uncompromising of Wilson's antileague foes. The senator possessed a sweet disposition, despite the leonine hair and shaggy brows that gave him the sobriquet of "the Lion of Idaho." He always managed to give the impression that whatever great cause he was thundering for or against—he was a very effective orator in an age that still appreciated oratory—he had taken the position solely on its merits. Despite the grave damage he inflicted on the Wilsonian covenant, the president continued to like and even admire him for his evangelical views and impersonal stands. Borah was a devilishly difficult opponent when he began speaking against the World Court, which he referred to as the league's court.

Just as difficult was his fellow anticourt orator, Senator Hiram Johnson of California, who had arrived in Washington only at the beginning of the Wilson administration's second term, in April 1917. Prior to that time, he had scarcely thought about international affairs. At that time, however, he took intense interest, and soon opposed Wilson's Russian policy. In this respect he was a conduit for the ideas of his friend, Colonel Raymond Robins, who had been to Russia with an American Red Cross mission in 1917–18. Johnson turned to opposing the league, in doing which he was second in importance only to Borah. He probably could have had the vice-presidential nomination of the Republican party in 1920, but refused it after failing to get the presidential nomination. In the 1920s he stood foursquare against the court. He was a less legalistic individual than Borah. His favorite method of attack was the appeal to patriotism, which he made with a leather-lunged oratory of an arm-waving, gesticulating variety that reminded contemporaries of the Reverend Billy Sunday, the retired baseball pitcher who had learned to preach the Gospel.

The reservations placed upon American consent to the court's protocol were inconsequential except for the fifth, regarding advisory opinions to the league council. This stated that the court should not, "without the consent of the United States, entertain any request for an advisory opinion touching any dispute or question in which the United States has or claims an interest." This was rejected by the other powers, so it proved necessary for the disappointed Elihu Root at the age of eighty-four to go to Geneva in 1929 and work out a formula for membership agreeable to the forty-eight nations which had adhered to the court protocol. The Root arrangements came up for a vote in the Senate in 1935 and narrowly failed, 52–36, seven votes short of the necessary two-thirds majority.

During the 1920s, while the debate raged in the Senate and throughout the country over joining the World Court, the governments of Harding and his successors gingerly commenced a modest cooperation with some of the organizations and bodies attached to the league in Geneva. Initially the Harding administration had not responded to league inquiries: letters from league officials were pigeon-holed as they came into the State Department. This fact at last came to the attention of Secretary of State Charles E. Hughes who took measures at least to acknowledge the existence of the league—and the offending department official was banished to a post in Egypt. By 1930, the United States had sent representatives to more than forty special league conferences on such nonpolitical subjects as communications and transit, general economics, counterfeiting of currency, codification of international law, and buoyage and lighting of coasts. Beginning in 1925, it sent an annual delegation to the almost interminable meetings of the Preparatory Commission for the Disarmament Conference, a league-sponsored effort to carry out the promises of the peace treaties that disarmament of the Central Powers should be only a first step to limitation of arms of all nations. But when the World Disarmament Conference opened in 1932, it promptly scrapped the projects drawn up earlier.

Groups that Worked for Peace

There was clearly great popular concern during the 1920s for maintaining world peace, a concern so strong that it could properly be described as a peace movement. Its antecedents of course reached back a long way before the 1920s, far beyond the hopes and despairs of the league supporters. Most of the American peace societies had been organized in the years after the War of 1812, but they were feeble organizations and languished after some years. In fact the interest in peace that was so notable many years later was hardly more than a flickering hope until the 1890s. The interest in arbitration, conciliation, and codification of international law then began to progress toward the assembling of Hague Conferences and the meeting in London in 1909 which sought to organize the international law of the sea. The outbreak of the war created a feeling of hopelessness; these efforts of the past had led only to the greatest war in history. But peace workers quickly took heart and throughout the great conflict planned for the organization of peace after the "war to end all war."

After the failure of the league covenant in the Senate, the American peace movement tended to diffuse its energies. The Harding administration managed momentarily to focus attention on the Washington Naval Conference, called to discuss limiting the size of navies, but uncertainty then reappeared. Private peace proposals after the conference looked either in the direction of abolishing war in one splendid gesture, or else in the traditional direction of a long, slow development of small but effective devices to limit war and bring it under control. Conservative peace organizations such as the Carnegie Endowment for International Peace and the World Peace Foundation, both founded in 1910, championed the World Court and codification of international law. They were joined by the peace committees of the World Council of Churches, the League of Nations Nonpartisan Association, the Woodrow Wilson Foundation, and other league-favoring groups.

Of a more urgent nature were the three or four dozen radical peace organizations in the United States that arose mostly at the end of the First World War. These groups sometimes were little more than the gatherings of one or two individuals with a vague following. But they partook of the perhaps basic American belief that if something needs to be changed the best way is to have an organization. There was the American Committee for the Outlawry of War, dominated by the Chicago lawyer Salmon O. Levinson who every morning dictated eight or ten effervescent letters to influential people. Levinson some years before had noted that in international law, war was neither legal nor illegal but nonlegal; he wished to make it illegal. Another group was Stop Organized Slaughter. There were the American Committee Against Militarism, the Fellowship of Reconciliation, the National Council for the Prevention of War. The latter group had been hastily organized to support the Washington Naval Conference, but its leader, a Congregational minister named Frederick J. Libby, afterward turned to other issues involving "the war system."

One of the fascinating aspects of the American peace movement during the decade was its attraction to women. Even before the war, Jane Addams had helped bring together the Women's International League for Peace and Freedom which was active throughout the 1920s. There were many other women in the peace movement, including Carrie Chapman Catt, a determined lady who was sometimes known as "that Catt woman." She had been involved in the suffrage movement, and won; the temperance movement, and won. Early in the 1920s she joined the peace movement. She asked for nothing less than the abolition of war. In the middle of an address in Cleveland, she threw down her notes and cried, "The women in this room can do this thing! The women in this room can do this thing!" Undaunted by individuals who did not believe she could succeed, she organized the

various national federations of women's clubs and groups —the League of Women Voters, the American Association of University Women, the Young Women's Christian Association. She federated these groups into the National Conference for the Cause and Cure of War, and the resultant stationery was impressive. She ran the names of her collaborative organizations down both sides of the letterhead. In subsequent years there occasionally would be a problem with some organization that wished to secede. When this sort of embarrassment arose, she would enter into a literary litigation, usually managing to keep the organization on the letterhead until, perhaps, that particular batch of stationery ran out.

Mrs Catt exerted unbearable pressure upon legislators who, in those early days of women's suffrage, were uncertain which way women would vote. Mrs Catt claimed to represent a solid phalanx of women voters. When on one occasion she asked to bring some ladies to the White House to present their opinions to President Calvin

Involvement in the European war disillusioned millions of Americans and led to the formation of antimilitary and pacifist organizations. These two posters were issued by the National Council for Limitation of Armaments (left) and World Peaceways.

Coolidge, her wishes were readily granted. Secretary of State Hughes sent a formal letter to Coolidge informing the president that Mrs Catt wished to bring a group of her supporters to call. Scrawled across the top in the unmistakable black-pen presidential handwriting, the present-day reader can see the answer: "Let 'em call."

Motives behind the Kellogg-Briand Pact

Perhaps the principal result of the American peace movement's confusion over programs proved to be the Kellogg-Briand Pact of 1928, in which virtually all countries of the world promised to abolish war and settle disputes by peaceful means. The origins and course of this fascinating declaration lay in the yearnings of the peace agitators and the peculiar needs of the foreign minister of France.

After the war France had been uncertain about how to ensure its security in relation to Germany. Successive cabinets during the 1920s depended upon a large French army, using the league as an anti-German coalition, and constructing a new alliance upon the ruins of the prewar system. This latter pursuit led directly to the Kellogg-Briand Pact. The French had signed agreements with Belgium (1920), Poland (1921), and Czechoslovakia (1924). In 1926 and 1927 they signed with the other two members of the Little Entente—Rumania and Yugoslavia. Public opinion in western Europe and elsewhere was hostile to alliances, considering them to be one of the prime causes of the recent war. The new alliances were therefore carefully labeled pacts of friendship and pacts of perpetual understanding. Moreover, the new League of Nations contained an inconvenient arrangement whereby all treaties had to be registered and their terms published. The French did not publish their agreement with Belgium which they said was only a military understanding. The other alliances possibly contained secret articles. The French were commonly said to suffer from "pactomania," never feeling secure against Germany.

In the later 1920s France was running out of possible allies. Russia was in the hands of the Bolsheviks, Britain was cool to any French connection, and in Europe there were only neutral states such as the Netherlands, untrustworthy states like Italy, and nonentities including Andorra, Monaco, and Liechtenstein. It is easy to imagine a certain desire to enlarge the alliance system by including the United States. Nicholas Murray Butler, president of Columbia University, who headed the Carnegie Endowment for International Peace, journeyed through Europe in 1926 and had a meeting with the French foreign minister, Aristide Briand. He told him how he had been reading the Prussian military scientist Clausewitz, who propounded the theory that war is an instrument of policy. Butler suggested that it would be worthwhile for France and the United States to abolish war between them. This was the proposal that Briand made to Secretary of State Frank B. Kellogg, Hughes's successor, on April 6, 1927, the tenth anniversary of America's entrance into the world war.

Kellogg was furious at first, rightly regarding the Briand proposal as a disguised request for a negative military alliance. (Briand was in effect asking for a pledge by the United States not to go to war in case France went to war with, say, Germany.) Kellogg could not state his objections publicly because, of course, the French foreign minister would have denied quasi-military motives. Undeterred, the French shamelessly enlisted the American peace movement against its own government; the peace leaders did not see Briand's purpose, only a large opportunity for peace, and put heavy pressure on the Coolidge administration. Kellogg sat on the proposal until December, when he no longer could hold out. He then turned the tables on Briand by asking him to extend the bilateral proposal to all nations—thereby making it worthless. Briand was embarrassed, for he could not publicly explain himself. Kellogg was humiliating him into a useless pact. He twisted and turned, wanting France and the United States to sign first, and eventually caved in. Meanwhile Kellogg, seventy-two years of age, commenced dreaming of doing something really big for world peace, and to the astonishment of his assistants began to covet the Nobel Peace Prize. The result was signature of the Kellogg-Briand Pact in Paris on August 27, 1928. Kellogg and Briand jointly received the Peace Prize in 1930, for what one cynical senator described as an international kiss.

The Washington Naval Conference

The most interesting area of diplomacy during the 1920s from the point of view of citizens of the United States was the grand effort to limit world armaments. In this regard Americans always thought of naval armaments, because the army had quickly dropped from its wartime strength of 4 million men to an insignificant figure, about 150,000 —which placed it somewhere below the size of the Portuguese army.

The idea of disarmament had always attracted Americans. They were fundamentally opposed to the standing armies of Europe, partly because their forebears had fled Europe to escape conscription, partly because the dominant English heritage in America considered standing armies repugnant to liberty. Of course, a large standing army made little sense for a nation with weak neighbors to north and south, and on east and west nothing but fish.

The idea of disarmament did not have serious attraction in Europe, however, until the last years of the nineteenth century when armaments, especially naval armaments, became very complex and a naval race was threatening. The race began in Europe at the turn of the century, between Britain and Germany. For prestige reasons the Americans were not far behind; the philosopher of navalism, Alfred Thayer Mahan, was an American. By the time of the First World War, the United States Navy ranked third in the world.

The war adjourned talk of disarmament, but the idea reappeared in the Fourteen Points of 1918 and in the Treaty of Versailles. Victory itself made naval disarmament a practical possibility, for the German fleet was scuttled. In May 1919, Admiral Sir Roger Keyes had shown Secretary of the Navy Josephus Daniels the interned German vessels at Scapa Flow, and pointed out that they were guarded by three trawlers. Shortly after, the trawlers were unnecessary.

Several factors pointed to the desirability of holding a naval disarmament conference. With the German fleet at the bottom of Scapa Flow it made little sense for the British, American, and Japanese navies to be so large. Furthermore, the cost of great fleets concerned American taxpayers and bothered the British and Japanese governments even more. Britain owed the United States a huge war debt. One-third of the Japanese budget in 1921 was going into armaments. In the United States the cost of the navy was the largest item in the national budget. And to the Harding administration, it seemed sensible to have a peace program to deflect the attention of the proleague lobby and the peace movement generally.

Finally, a naval disarmament conference would provide an opportunity for the United States and Britain to bring the Japanese government to account for its expansionist policy in the western Pacific. The Anglo-American effort would try to force an end to the expansion of the Japanese Navy, which had been increasing too rapidly for their tastes. They could raise the problem of China, which had proved so awkward during the Paris Peace Conference and might better be discussed in a small group. It might be possible to trade off a general settlement in the Far East for a limit on the Japanese Navy. The British had an alliance with the Japanese that bothered some Americans, who did not realize that the London government had so qualified its support of the alliance that the latter could not possibly have been directed against the United States. A conference on naval arms would provide a chance to discuss the alliance and perhaps eliminate it.

The conference opened in Washington on November 12, 1921. It was attended by delegates from nine countries— the United States, Britain, France, Italy, Japan, Belgium, China, the Netherlands, and Portugal. The first session involved the most surprising diplomatic coup of the decade. Secretary Hughes had not merely decided upon

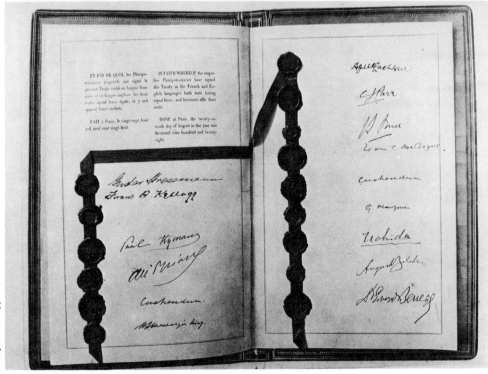

What the French foreign minister, Aristide Briand, intended to be a bilateral peace pledge between France and the United States was transformed by America's secretary of state, Frank B. Kellogg, into a multinational declaration aimed at outlawing war throughout the world. Above: The secretary signs the Kellogg-Briand Pact in Paris, 1928. Left: One of the pages of the treaty bears the signatures and seals of the world leaders who endorsed the pact.

the American program for limitation and reduction—he offered it to the delegates during the first meeting.

International conferences traditionally began with welcoming speeches of a soporific nature, and President Harding duly opened with an elegant "bloviation." He was followed by Hughes, as principal negotiator for the host country. The secretary began with the usual high-flown remarks, allowing his audience of diplomats to relax in their comfortable chairs in the Pan-American building. The reporters relaxed over their pencils. In the middle of the speech he repeated the old bromide about competition in armaments, "There is only one adequate way out and that is to end it now." No one thought anything of the remark. Then, suddenly, he began to set out the American program in great detail, listing not merely the eleven ships of his own country which were to be

broken up but vessels of the fleets of Britain, France, Italy, and Japan. He called for destruction of sixty-six battleships. The atmosphere became electric. Reporters' pencils were almost audible in their furious scribblings. The reporter Mark Sullivan looked down from the gallery at the hero of Jutland, Admiral Sir David Beatty, who "came forward in his chair with the manner of a bulldog, sleeping on a sunny doorstep, who has been poked in the stomach by the impudent foot of an itinerant soap-canvasser seriously lacking in any sense of the most ordinary proprieties or considerations of personal safety."

Consternation reigned. When Hughes finished, applause roared from the onlookers and some of the delegates. Cries arose of "Briand! Briand!", demanding the French premier. Thinking his name had been called, old William Jennings Bryan, present as a reporter, moistened his lips and half stood up, saying aloud to William Allen White who sat next to him, "Shall I speak? Shall I speak?" White yanked furiously on Bryan's coattails and almost shouted in reply, "Sit down you fool!" Concerned for their own exigencies, the leading delegates had begun to rise and support the American secretary of state.

The 1921–22 Washington conference agreed, among other things, to limit naval strength. Shown from left are the Big Four delegates: Japan's Prince Tokugawa, Lord Balfour of Britain, Secretary of State Charles E. Hughes, and Briand of France.

Brown Brothers

The subsequent work of the conference was anti-climactic. There were three principal treaties agreed to. The naval pact was the Five-Power Treaty, under the terms of which the major naval powers of the world limited their battleships and aircraft carriers according to a ratio that a newspaperman described as 5-5-3-1.75-1.75. The numbers stood roughly for hundreds of thousands of battleship tonnage for Britain, the United States, Japan, France, and Italy respectively. The Japanese, unhappy with their tonnage as compared to the figures for the British and Americans, soon were saying that the 5-5-3 part of the ratio was equivalent to Rolls Royce-Rolls Royce-Ford. Japanese critics of this agreement chalked the three numbers on walls of buildings throughout Japan. Permitted carrier tonnage for the powers was considerably less, and it had been included to prevent conversion of battleship hulls to carriers.

The Four-Power Treaty, consisting of the naval powers less Italy, undertook to preserve peace in the Far East and promised that in event of trouble the signatories would "communicate with each other as to the most efficient measures to be taken, jointly or singly, to meet the exigencies of the particular situation." The treaty served as a dignified replacement of the recently terminated Anglo-Japanese Alliance which had troubled Anglo-American relations. It was a decent burial. The American delegate Elihu Root declared of the Four-Power Treaty: "I doubt if any formal treaty ever accomplished so much by doing so little." It operated on the well-known diplomatic principle that the way to make an agreement useless is to widen the signatories, the presumption being that four nations were less likely to be cooperative than two—borne out by the Kellogg-Briand Pact which was to include almost all nations of the world and be almost completely futile.

The third major agreement to come out of the Washington conference was the Nine-Power Treaty, signed by all states present. This pact committed the signatories to the Open Door principles which Secretary of State John Hay propounded at the turn of the century. This involved respect for equal commercial opportunity in China and recognition of that nation's sovereignty, independence, and territorial integrity. Several lesser agreements were made at the conference, among them an arrangement between the Chinese and Japanese, at which Secretary Hughes and British Foreign Secretary Lord Balfour acted as intermediaries. In this agreement the Japanese consented to leave the Shantung Peninsula and in other ways to respect Chinese sovereignty. They also agreed to withdraw from Siberia, where they had had forces stationed since 1918, and restore to Russia the northern half of Sakhalin Island.

In later years, especially as peace collapsed in the Far East during the 1930s, much criticism gathered around the Washington agreements. To many observers before and after the Second World War, Hughes seemed to have mistaken the fervor of the peace movement for serious thought regarding world peace; it seemed his actions had been not merely hasty but futile.

The Republican party's platform in 1924, for obvious reasons, had announced the Five-Power Treaty as "the greatest peace document ever drawn." But the friends of the navy had begun to criticize the treaties even before the statesmen had signed them. The Navy League kept up a clamor throughout the 1920s. When the Japanese Army occupied Manchuria in 1931–33 and fighting broke out between Japan and the Chinese in 1937, the approval surrounding the Washington conference virtually disappeared. By the time Hughes, now Chief Justice, retired from the Supreme Court in 1941, the criticisms of the Washington conference had turned into acrimony. It was said that Hughes simply had arranged a disarmament of the American and British fleets, and allowed the Japanese a respite until the 1930s when they chose to build beyond the Washington limits. The Japanese later fortified the mandated former German island groups in the Pacific—the Marianas, Marshalls, and Carolines—creating in effect unsinkable aircraft carriers against which a weakened American fleet, seeking to fight its way from Pearl Harbor to the Philippines, would have grave difficulty. The Five-Power Treaty meanwhile had prevented the British from fortifying Hong Kong and the Americans from bolstering the defenses of Guam and the Philippines.

Against the near torrent of criticism that afterward surrounded Hughes it must be said that, given the pacific nature of the 1920s, a far different decade from the one that followed, the Washington agreements made a good deal of sense. Navies needed to be reduced. Moreover, the agreement of 1922 applied mainly to battleships, which had been doomed after Jutland if not before. Carriers were something else; but in the 1920s the carrier-based plane had not yet revealed all its military capacities and it is unfair to blame the statesmen of the time for not foreseeing its future military importance.

The peaceable sentiments of people everywhere, not merely in America but in Europe and even in Japan, needed reinforcement by a conference of the leading powers that included the United States. The conference amounted to a testimony by the American government that whatever lack of wisdom characterized its policy toward the league and toward the major diplomatic problems of Europe during the 1920s, it was interested in making at least one sizable contribution to world peace. In the Far East, Japan was a peaceful nation, not the military aggressor of the following decade. The Japanese had profited greatly from the world war and were enjoying a modest economic prosperity. The political lesson of the war had been the triumph of democracy, and the Japanese government looked toward democratic development. If that lesson later was lost, it was because of the

Great Depression and other factors unrelated to the success of the Washington Naval Conference.

The work of the conference was completed in 1927 and in 1930, in discussions at Geneva and London. After the Washington conference a quiet naval race had begun in categories of vessels not limited by the Five-Power Treaty, in particular cruisers. The Washington treaty had defined a battleship as any vessel over 10,000 tons displacement and carrying guns of a caliber larger than eight inches. In the minds of American admirals this definition produced the possibility of a superior type of cruiser, the largest vessel allowable under the treaty. By the end of the decade the American navy, which had not commissioned any cruisers between 1908 and 1922, began to commission so-called "heavy" cruisers. The Japanese followed, and so did the British, the latter with great reluctance as they possessed large numbers of smaller cruisers which supposedly would be outfought by the new class of "treaty cruisers." The absurdity of this cruiser race was that the only way to test the new vessels was to assess them in battle, presumably the very course that the disarmament conferences were trying to avoid. The issues involved were discussed without result at the Geneva conference of 1927, but in 1930 at London the matter was settled. An arrangement was made to extend the Washington naval ratios to include the lesser types of craft, cruisers and destroyers and submarines. This was done arbitrarily by "discounting" light cruisers against heavies in determining total cruiser tonnage for the purpose of limitation. The conference also gave Japan a destroyer ratio of 3.5 to the Anglo-American 5, and parity in submarines.

When the Washington ratios were abandoned in the mid-1930s, an element of order in international relations disappeared. It was a pity that the cooperation on navies had not extended to land forces and in particular German land forces, for German rearmament in the mid-1930s became the basic unsettling factor in world diplomacy. But in the 1920s, when it looked as if the tides of world prosperity would wash away the passions of the world war, there was not sufficient understanding—there was only the emotionalism of the peace movement which lacked any real, logical underpinning. By the time statesmen realized how insecure the world's peace had been, how fragile all their arrangements were, the time for international cooperation had slipped beyond their grasp. The economic chaos of the Great Depression brought baleful new leaders in Germany, and twisted the leadership in Italy. Rearmament became the only feasible policy for the democracies of the West.

King George V formally opens the 1930 London naval conference. The Washington limits on battleships were extended to include destroyers, cruisers, and submarines.

Paying off the War

The diplomacy of the United States during the 1920s also involved economic issues. These centered upon the reparations European nations collected, or tried to collect, from Germany, and the debts they owed the United States. If there was any original sin involved in the money dispute that raged across the Atlantic throughout the 1920s

and 1930s, it was European rather than American. The Europeans, especially the French, were intent on collecting money from Germany, and in retrospect it was a mistake for them to have tried to do so by writing reparations into the Treaty of Versailles. There was of course precedent for reparations; and the Allies deserved reparations. The German army had devastated northern France in 1914–18, the farmlands pocked with huge shell holes, towns and villages reduced to rubble, mines flooded. Germany should have paid. Nonetheless the Germans did

not want to pay, and it was a mistake to try to force them.

A secondary error in the money argument was also European, namely the decision in all the chancelleries of the Allies that there would be no more money paid to the United States in war debts than Europe collected from Germany. Britain's foreign secretary, Balfour, made this point in 1922: "In no circumstances do we propose to ask more from our debtors than is necessary to pay our creditors." It was an unfortunate observation. During the war the Europeans had promised to repay their borrow-

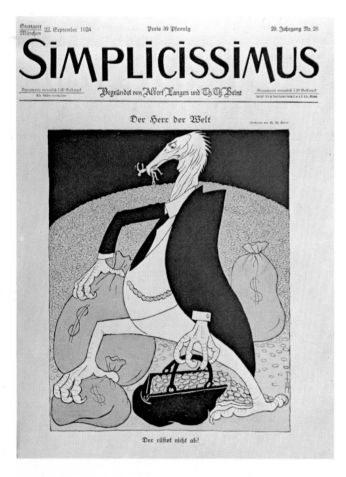

Reparation payments due from Germany were a source of contention in the 1920s. Above left: A German cartoon portrays the victorious Allies as a money-grubbing ogre bent on plunder. Above right: This American drawing suggests that Germany was more wealthy than she admitted. Opposite: Financier Charles G. Dawes chaired the international bankers' conference on reparation payments.

ings from the United States, and with good reason Americans took to heart the supposed remark of President Coolidge that ''They hired the money, didn't they?''

But America was not blameless. Whatever the disastrous consequences of recent European actions, the government of the United States should not have insisted on payment of the debts—the $7 billion lent during the war together with the $3.2 billion lent for reconstruction afterwards. It was too fond a hope of the American people that they would be able to collect international debts in such unprecedented amounts.

The United States government twisted and turned in its efforts to collect, without much result except to incur the ill will of all the European governments. The Americans sought to keep the reparations and war debts accounts separate, refusing to acknowledge any connection. To do so would have put the Americans in the role of recipients of both. Slowly the Treasury made arrangements to scale down the rate of interest on the war debts, which had been fixed at 5 per cent, which seemed too high to maintain over a long period of time. The interest was cut drastically, according to capacity to pay. The British rate was reduced in 1923 to 3.3 per cent, the French (1926) to 1.6 per cent, the Italian (1925) to 0.4 per cent. These three accounts comprised over 90 per cent of the total of funded debts. The renegotiated obligations were payable

over sixty-two years. Principal plus interest on the war debts over that period would have totaled more than $22 billion.

To ensure repayment it proved necessary to take part in two European conferences between the German government and the countries to which the Germans owed reparations. The Americans found themselves virtually forced into negotiations with the Germans over reparation payments. In 1924 a bankers' committee met in London under the chairmanship of the American banker Charles G. Dawes. An agreement was negotiated with Germany which was then ratified by a meeting of government representatives. The Dawes Plan put reparations on an annual schedule. An international loan of $200 million was immediately floated, and United States banks took up $110 million of the total. But subscriptions within America exceeded $1 billion, so that the banks had to make allotments among the eager applicants.

The Young Plan of 1929, named after its organizer, the American financier Owen D. Young, reduced the original estimate of reparations, put tentatively in 1921 by the Reparations Commission at $33 billion plus interest, to about $26 billion including principal and interest. It divided annual payments into two categories, absolute and conditional, the latter depending on the achievement of German prosperity.

Negotiation of the Dawes and Young plans had the enthusiastic backing of American bankers because at this time they were busy making loans to Germany—which about equaled the total reparation payments, which in turn were related to the war debt payments, a nice circular exercise. The bankers lent funds to the German government, to industry, and to municipal projects. The loans increased markedly in the latter half of the decade as prosperity returned to Germany. The flow of American money continued until the last years of the 1920s, when even the high German interest rates proved less attractive than the opportunities of putting money into the New York stock market.

With the beginning of the Great Depression the reparations-war debts arrangement, a structure that had been erected with what seemed enormous calculation, was buffeted and pushed and pulled until, in 1931–32, it came tumbling down in ruins. Shortly after the Young Plan went into operation, the world economic depression

began with the stock market crash in America and spread quickly to Europe and the rest of the world. The most industrialized economies, the most highly capitalized, were quickly hit. Soon reparation payments slowed, and at the insistence of American and European bankers they were then stopped—because continued payment would have stripped the gold backing from Germany's currency and made repayment of the bankers' private loans virtually impossible.

It had become evident that the structure of international finance in Germany was in grave danger. American bankers in the 1920s often had borrowed short and lent long to build housing developments, stadiums, and municipal projects of various sorts in Germany. It was impossible to pull funds out of such projects and repay the short-term loans floated in the United States. So long as the interest payments continued, bankers had not looked too hard at what their German friends were doing with the money.

By the summer of 1931 all this miscalculation produced immense pressure for the United States government to arrange a "standstill" on both reparations and war debts. Total estimates of private American funds lent Germany reached $2.25 billion. A horrified President Herbert Hoover then discovered that billions of additional dollars were floating in Europe in virtually unsecured trade bills and completely unsecured bank acceptances. These perhaps equally uncollectable debts had not been figured in the first estimates of American funds lent to Germany. Trade bills and bank acceptances in Central Europe amounted to $5 billion, of which American banks held more than $1.7 billion. After hurried negotiation, in which the French government dragged its heels and gave the impression it desired the German economy to collapse, a moratorium on reparations and war debts and a standstill on trade bills and bank acceptances were arranged in July 1931. The standstill on bills and acceptances was extended by subsequent agreements until 1940 when these short-term credits advanced by American banks had been reduced by various devices to less than $40 million.

Beginning a year from July 1931, reparations and war debts nominally commenced to run once more, though in actuality the payments were virtually halted. Reparations ended first. The Allied governments which were debtors to the United States met at Lausanne in the summer of 1932 and proposed a more than 90 per cent reduction of German reparations, conditional on a similar slashing of the war debts. The Germans immediately saw that the Allies were disinclined to collect further reparations, and defaulted. To no avail, the American government indignantly refused to cancel the war debts owed to it. But the Allies either defaulted when debt payments were scheduled to resume, in December 1932, or promised to default on the next six-month payment, in

June 1933, when only Finland paid in full.

The period of American foreign relations that began with the victory of the Republicans in the presidential election of 1920 had managed to give the impression of stability until the world economy collapsed under the weight of the Great Depression.

Among the causes of the depression was the failure of the American, German, and especially British economies to allow for adjustments among themselves as they began to compete during the later nineteenth century. No one thought much about international economic cooperation, so long as things ran along from year to year. A reckoning had to come. The expansion of national economies was too rapid and too great. It was impossible to keep money payments running in the proper directions to prop up the structure from problem to problem.

Furthermore, the American and European economies had been dislocated by the First World War. The conflict forced expansion of munitions industries and other war-connected enterprises and set off inflation in all countries. There was a failure to create better world economic con-

ditions in the 1920s, when almost everything was run on a national basis. If an economy revealed some minor trouble, import quotas, tariffs, or subsidies were applied. Money payments from country to country were mere paper transactions year after year. All the while a rigid situation prevailed in national currencies, with fixed exchange rates and, in many countries, very thin gold reserves. By the end of the decade the wartime experience of many Americans in bond-buying, in the Liberty Bond drives, and the Victory Bond campaign, had translated itself into the heady business of stock-speculation which ran up prices on the New York Stock Exchange. The crash of October 1929 followed, and soon spread throughout the world.

In retrospect it can be seen that there was no economic wisdom to draw upon, and that past precedents were almost entirely of no value. Secretary of the Treasury

Andrew Mellon looked upon the depression almost with relish. He thought it would be healthy for the economy, and lead to a shaking out of weak businesses as had happened in previous economic downturns. No wisdom came from any government, American or European. By 1932–33 the result was near chaos. Gloomy prognostications about the decline of the West suddenly became popular. People remembered that the economist John Maynard Keynes had seen grave economic flaws in the peace settlement of 1919, and reflected that (as the historian Arnold Toynbee wrote) the major mistake of the 1920s was to think that the problems of the decade had been solely political.

And so the golden years of the 1920s which began in hope ended in disillusion. In this period it had proved impossible to set the foundations for world peace. The enormous efforts of the Allies for victory in 1914–18 came crashing down in the cataclysm of world economic depression, and out of that utter confusion would come another world war and a train of international calamities that runs on today.

At Lausanne in 1932, America's European debtors proposed to slash German reparations if their own war debts were similarly cut. This photo shows some of the delegates, among them Germany's von Neurath (second from left) and von Papen (third from left) with Premier Herriot of France next to him. Britain's Ramsay MacDonald lights a cigar.

Erich Salomon/John Hillelson Agency

Chapter 2

TOWARD UNITY IN THE HEMISPHERE

Military intervention by the United States in Latin America and the Caribbean was nothing new, but the dispatch of marines in 1926–27 to quell civil war in Nicaragua proved ineffective and led to a change in course. President Hoover's "Good Neighbor" policy announced an end to armed intervention and stressed the desire to settle problems by peaceful means—a policy his successor endorsed as well. The "big stick" gave way to the benign eye, replacing suspicion and ill will with a measure of trust in American motives. Relations with Canada also changed for the better as coolness and independent action were transformed into warmth and cooperation. By 1941, a foundation had been laid for solidarity in the American continent.

The Good Neighbor Policy

American policy in the Western Hemisphere between the world wars is really two policies, two separate histories. Relations with Canada were very different from those with the Latin American republics. For one thing, Canada had never been a member of the Pan American Union, formed in 1889 by the republics of the Western Hemisphere. As a member of the British Commonwealth of Nations, Canada was regarded in Washington as, at best, a part of the European system of states against which the Monroe Doctrine had been directed. In 1918, it remained in some ways less than fully independent from the British Crown, and it was not thought of as an "American Republic," as that term was understood in the United States Department of State. As late as 1936, Assistant Secretary of State Sumner Welles is reported as saying that "there is no more logical reason why Canada should be represented in the Pan American Union than Jamaica . . . or British, French or Dutch Guiana." It was a real question whether Canada at that time was a part of the political, as distinct from the geographic, Western Hemisphere.

Although the United States was a member of the Pan American Union, its relations with Latin America were more complicated and difficult than those with Canada. No less than twenty times between 1898 and 1920, the United States sent soldiers or marines to enforce its demands on governments or rebels in countries of the Caribbean and Central America. In some countries the troops remained only for days or weeks; but in others including Cuba, Haiti, the Dominican Republic, and Nicaragua, occupations lasted for a decade or more.

The traditional justification for such use of force was the Monroe Doctrine of 1823, whose "fundamental concept" as interpreted by Secretary of State Frank B. Kellogg in 1929 was "the peace and safety of the Western Hemisphere through the absolute political separation of Europe from the countries of this Western World." The doctrine had been modified in the early 1900s by the Roosevelt Corollary. If Caribbean countries defaulted on obligations to European citizens or governments, said President Theodore Roosevelt, the United States might use force to prevent interventions by European governments and to make arrangements such as collection of customs duties, so that creditors—both European and American—might get their money back. Other official justifications for intervention included protection of the lives and property of United States citizens, and the endeavor to encourage political stability and implantation of democratic institutions in Caribbean societies.

A subsystem of international relations was thus created in which the United States regarded itself as legally and morally authorized to intervene militarily in its neighbors'

affairs for various reasons—all defined by itself. This system disintegrated in the decade after the First World War, when a new set of relationships developed under the name of the Good Neighbor policy.

A major result of the First World War for the Americas, was the elimination of the slightest threat of intervention in Latin America by any European or Asiatic country. The Monroe Doctrine lost its credibility, although this was not immediately appreciated. So long as interventions remained short, cheap, and easily carried out by executive action alone, it was possible, as in Honduras in 1924, to land marines to protect "the American Minister and American colony," because "a condition of anarchy seems likely to develop." However, in Nicaragua in 1926, when another intervention was undertaken, the operation turned out to be long, big, and expensive. And the old justifications for the use of force were now rejected by Latin Americans, who had been bitterly protesting them for years. Suddenly, and far more importantly, they were joined by strong and vocal sectors of American public opinion including influential members of Congress, such as Senators William E. Borah and George W. Norris.

Intervention in Nicaragua

A civil war in Nicaragua provided the occasion for United States intervention. The United States and other governments recognized the dubiously elected conservative President Adolfo Díaz; Mexico recognized the liberal civilian leader Juan Sacasa, and probably gave him support in the form of military supplies. The liberals, led in the field by General José Moncada, were on the point of defeating the conservative forces when, on December 23, 1926, US Marines landed at Puerto Cabezas, Sacasa's headquarters. Shortly afterwards they were protecting Díaz in the capital of Managua. President Calvin Coolidge, in a message to Congress, referred to Sacasa's "Mexican allies" and justified use of the marines by expressing his "deep concern" at "any serious threat to stability and constitutional government in Nicaragua tending toward anarchy and jeopardizing American interests, especially if such state of affairs is contributed to or brought about by outside influences or by any foreign power." Was the Monroe Doctrine about to be applied to Mexico?

The "foreign power" was obviously Mexico, although an official spokesman hinted darkly at "Bolshevism." For about two weeks there was a "war scare," exacerbated by Mexico's plans for expropriation of valuable agricultural lands held by United States citizens. However, a great protest by thousands of Americans, organized by the National Council for Prevention of War and the Federal Council of the Churches of Christ, and the passage

President Coolidge ordered marines into Nicaragua in December 1926 when rebel forces were on the point of overthrowing the conservative government. Below: A battalion arrives at Matagalpa in 1927. Inset: US Marines patrol the streets of Managua after an earthquake in 1931.

American marines remained in Nicaragua for six years. Intervention had been undertaken in order to restore political stability to the region. This photograph shows United States personnel fighting a fire in Managua.

of a Senate resolution on January 25, 1927, by a vote of 79–0 favoring arbitration of the expropriation dispute, persuaded Coolidge to choose peaceful settlement of the issue with Mexico. Indicative of the depth of feeling on the matter was the *New York Times*'s encouraging statement of January 12 that Coolidge was "the last man to imagine cherishing the thought of riding through slaughter to a throne."

Coolidge had no annexationist aims anywhere in Latin America, and he did not wish to become responsible for any bloodshed in Nicaragua of marines or liberals. He sent Henry L. Stimson as his special representative to study the situation, and Stimson's conclusions were accepted in Washington. These stated that free elections in Central America were the key to solving the political problem there; such elections in Nicaragua would have to be supervised by marines for a substantial period of time; during this period, the marines would train a local constabulary (National Guard) that could later assure the continuance of free elections. These conclusions were also accepted by all but one of the leaders of the Nicaraguan civil war in the agreement of Tipitapa, negotiated underneath a large blackthorn tree and dated May 4, 1927. The first supervised election, held in the autumn of 1928, resulted in General Moncada becoming president.

The election was held peaceably enough, but the

troubles were not over. General César Augusto Sandino, opposed to the presence of US Marines under any circumstances, had rejected the Tipitapa agreement and, with some 400 followers, had taken to the mountains. For five years he directed guerrilla raids, eluding the marines and escaping from their air strikes—the first use of airpower in the history of the Americas. When hard pressed, he slipped across the border into Honduras where the marines could not follow. His raids killed a number of Nicaraguans, and some fifteen United States citizens in lumber camps. United States officials called Sandino a "bandit" and compared him to "the savages who fell upon American settlers in our country 150 years ago." But in Latin America and elsewhere he was regarded as a brave man, defying the power of a hated foreign nation in the cause of Nicaragua's independence.

Sandino played a major role in bringing about a momentous change in United States policy in the Caribbean. Implicitly, the government of the United States

recognized that it had failed to protect its own citizens in Nicaragua by intervention and the use of force. This was the first such failure in the small countries of the Caribbean and Central America. Cuba, Haiti, and the Dominican Republic had earlier been pacified, and other interventions had been brief and simple. By the spring of 1931, however, Stimson, then secretary of state in the administration of President Herbert Hoover, declared that the United States could not provide "general protection of Americans in Nicaragua" because of unacceptable difficulties and commitments. He advised Americans in Nicaragua to go to coastal towns where they could be protected or evacuated by the navy, since regular troops could not operate effectively against "outlaws." Stimson

Marine corps officers prepare to take to the air. Continued uprisings in Nicaragua brought home to the United States the difficulty of safeguarding American citizens and property there.

claimed that the Nicaraguan National Guard, by then 2,100 strong, could take care of the bandits. He had already announced that all US Marines would be withdrawn from Nicaragua following the supervised election of 1932.

The withdrawal took place in early 1933 just before the inauguration of President Franklin D. Roosevelt. It was accompanied by the Department of State's claims that it had fulfilled its part of the Tipitapa agreement by supervising two fair elections, and by training the National Guard, which was described as "an efficient organization . . . with a high *esprit de corps*," whose nonpolitical character both political parties intended to preserve. Sacasa became president in the 1932 elections, and General Anastasio Somoza became head of the National Guard. In 1934, on Somoza's orders, Sandino was murdered by members of the guard, and in 1936, Somoza was elected president, an office he and his family have continued to hold into the 1970s in well-controlled, unsupervised elections.

Augusto Sandino led opponents of the American presence in Nicaragua. Below: The rebels lay an ambush. Inset: The diminutive Sandino said in 1927: "I want a free country or death." He was killed in 1934, a year after the marines had left.

Culver Pictures. Inset: Marine Corps Photo, National Archives

The nearly total failure of the United States in Nicaragua, either to protect American citizens or to change the basic character of Nicaraguan politics, resulted in a drastic reconsideration of Washington's policies in the Caribbean. Stimson found that he was being criticized at home and abroad as being responsible for the presence of marines in Nicaragua at the same time that he was criticizing what he confided to his diary as Japan's "monstrous work" in Manchuria. Morally and practically, the Nicaraguan policy was in ruins. In terms of policy, as *The Times* of London commented in 1931: "A reversal of the methods and theories of the Coolidge period is under way."

The Good Neighbor Policy

The reversal, begun in the administration of Herbert Hoover, was completed in 1938 at the Lima Conference of American States. The extent of the about-face may be seen by comparing two texts—one from a speech by former Secretary of State Charles Evans Hughes at Havana in 1928 and the other from an agreement signed by Secretary of State Cordell Hull in 1938 at the Lima conference. Hughes's speech included this passage:

> What are we going to do when [a foreign] government breaks down and American citizens are in danger of their lives? Are we to stand by and see them killed because a government in circumstances which it cannot control and for which it may not be responsible can no longer afford reasonable protection? . . . Now it is a principle of international law that in such a case a government is fully justified in taking action—I would call it interposition of a temporary character—for the purpose of protecting the lives and property of its nationals.

But ten years later, Hull endorsed the following: "No state has the right to intervene in the internal or external affairs of another."

After his election in 1928, Hoover had made a good-will journey to a number of South American countries, in part to try to overcome some of the ill will that had been expressed against the United States by Latin American governments. Hoover stated publicly that "it ought not to be the policy of the United States to intervene by force to secure or maintain contracts between our citizens and foreign states or their citizens." He affirmed that he wished "to maintain not only the cordial relations of governments with each other but the relations of *good neighbors.*" Under Hoover the United States withdrew marines from Nicaragua, did not intervene in Cuba despite provocations and treaty rights, and recognized Central American governments that came into power by revolution in the early depression years.

The new Roosevelt administration regarded the Nicaraguan affair as a blunder. One of its principles was to be, in Hull's words, "religious adherence to the principle of nonintervention." Yet it soon found itself in such a situation in Cuba that it barely could avoid intervention in the form of another marine landing.

In the 1920s and at least until 1937, "hemispheric unity" was not a policy of the United States. It was not trying to annex or confederate with any of its neighbors; it had no sense of a need for unity; there was no external threat. Coolidge automatically followed established policy in Nicaragua. Stimson modified the policy and retired under a smoke screen of claimed "success." He ran into insoluble problems with Sandino's all-out defiance and with the US Senate's refusal to appropriate funds to send more marines to supervise the 1932 election. Moreover, antiintervention, antiimperialist, propeace, and pro-League of Nations forces were vocal in their opposition. Stimson sought not hemispheric unity, but a refuge from harassment at home, in Nicaragua, and abroad.

Roosevelt's inaugural speech dedicated the United States "to the policy of Good Neighbor—the neighbor who respects his obligations and respects the sanctity of his agreements in and with a world of neighbors." The president was developing views he had expressed in an article in 1928 in *Foreign Affairs.* "The outside world views us with less good will today than at any previous period," he wrote at that time. Recent policy "has allowed a dislike and mistrust of long standing to grow into something like positive hate and fear." Therefore, "single-handed intervention by us in the internal affairs of other nations must end; with the cooperation of others we shall have more order in this hemisphere and less dislike." The transformation of hatred into friendship and cooperation with Latin American countries, both in maintaining order and in the growth of trade, was the strongest element in Roosevelt's thinking at the outset of his first administration. In terms of principled action consistently followed, the Good Neighbor policy was shaped in the Roosevelt administrations between 1933 and 1941.

Policy Toward Cuba and Nicaragua

In Cuba in 1923, the enemies of President Gerardo Machado's dictatorial regime defied his martial law with bombings and terrorism. The situation had been growing more violent and Machado's suppression more harsh since 1929, but Secretary Stimson, scarred from Nicaragua, refused to intervene militarily. He refused despite the provisions of the Platt Amendment, ratified in 1903, that the United States might intervene in Cuba for "the maintenance of a government adequate for the protection of life, property, and individual liberty." Entering office with the conviction that Coolidge had bungled in Nicaragua, Roosevelt and Hull were confident they could intermeddle or interpose pacifically in Cuba to give "friendly assistance and advice" to the Cuban people so that new and fair elections might be held and the disorder ended. Sumner Welles arrived in Havana on May 8, 1933, intending, in his own words, to prevent "conditions which lead to political disturbances, revolution, and civil war," and so to avoid "measures of coercion"—intervention—after a civil outbreak.

Welles had a momentary success. Intriguing with the Cuban secretary of war, General Alberto Herrera, he arranged for Machado to leave Cuba on August 12, on a "temporary leave of absence"—which turned out to be permanent. Herrera, becoming president, instantly resigned and named Machado's secretary of state, Carlos Manuel de Céspedes, to succeed him. Welles was congratulated by Roosevelt and Hull, but the glow of achievement lasted for less than a month. Céspedes was overthrown on September 5 by soldiers and noncommissioned officers of the army, who deposed their officers and set up a revolutionary junta of five civilians. A professor of biology in the University of Havana, Ramón Grau San Martín, headed the junta.

Within three days, Welles made three separate

Roosevelt and Secretary Cordell Hull believed the Nicaraguan intervention had been a mistake. In his inaugural address, the new president pledged America to "the policy of the Good Neighbor."

Library of Congress

proposals to Washington for the landing of troops. While the fighting between officers and men was proceeding, Welles requested a landing by marines aboard the destroyer *McFarland.* Hull replied that unless Welles were himself in physical danger, he should not insist on this request. Later, he asked for "a limited intervention," involving the landing of troops to assist a new government and help organize a new army. Finally, claiming that "complete anarchy" existed throughout the country, Welles asked Washington to provide "the moral assistance a small number of Marines would create." Such action, he said, would not be "a military intervention" but only a "police service." In reply, Welles received an emphatic, personal telephone message from Roosevelt that terminated his efforts at intervention.

Roosevelt did take the precautionary measure of sending naval vessels, including the battleship *Mississippi,* but ordered them to remain over the horizon, out of sight of Havana. He would have intervened only if there had arisen imminent danger to the lives of American citizens. (One American was killed in the disorders, but he was apparently shot unintentionally while watching the siege by army officers of the Hotel Nacional in downtown Havana.) Hull stated that there would be no intervention were brought to bear by Welles, who was recalled in November 1933, and by his successor, Jefferson Caffery, to make it impossible for the Grau San Martín regime to continue in power. Recognition, and therefore a sugar quota, was refused by Roosevelt. Welles and Caffery talked with Fulgencio Batista, who had led the mutiny against Céspedes, about the installation of a new president. Formally, the United States considered that recognition should be witheld until there was evidence that Grau San Martín had popular support, and was able to maintain law and order. Informally, Welles believed that a "social

Left: Fulgencio Batista played a leading part in the overthrow of Cuba's President Céspedes in 1933. Below: Batista, the new army chief, addresses a crowd in Havana after the military coup.

unless absolutely unavoidable: "If we have to go in there again, we will never be able to come out." He also told Welles: "I am telling people who have property there to let it be injured a little," thus in effect accepting and extending the implications of the policy of Stimson in Nicaragua, who had written in his diary that Americans in Nicaragua "were a pampered lot of people" who thought they had "a right to call for troops" whenever any danger threatened.

There was no direct intervention. But strong pressures

revolution" was being undertaken by Grau San Martín. And Caffery asserted that the regime had "seemingly communistic tendencies," and was supported only by the army and by "ignorant masses" who were "misled by utopian promises."

When Batista finally decided it would be safe for him to withdraw his support from Grau San Martín he gave it to Carlos Mendieta, an experienced politician. Grau resigned on January 15, 1934. Mendieta was installed on the eighteenth and five days later his government was recognized by Washington. Intervention had been avoided, but what may be called interference or intermeddling had brought intervention perilously close and had important political consequences in subsequent Cuban history.

The lesson drawn from this intense Cuban experience was clear: if the United States intended not to intervene, it should refrain from the kind of political interference that had become customary on the part of its ambassadors in Caribbean republics. This conclusion was formally embodied in an important instruction sent by the Department of State to its ministers on April 30, 1936. The instruction, signed by Cordell Hull, stated that the United States was now "in the fullest sense, applying the Good Neighbor policy to Central America." This policy was incompatible, it said, with the involvement of the United States government "in the domestic concerns of any of the Central American republics." Ministers were instructed to decline to give any advice to Central American officials on any domestic question, even when such advice might be sought. In the past, it had been found "that such advice rapidly came to be considered as intervention, and, in fact, sometimes terminated in actual intervention." Consequently, "doubtful assistance" was rendered to those governments, and relations between the United States and Latin American governments were damaged.

This policy of abstention from interference as well as from intervention was applied throughout the Caribbean area. For example, when President Sacasa of Nicaragua sent a delegation to Washington to seek aid against the presidential ambitions of General Somoza, on the ground that the United States had responsibility for the actions of the National Guard which it had created, both aid and advice were rejected. When the leader of the delegation regretted that Willard L. Beaulac of the Department of State "hesitated" to give advice, Beaulac gaily answered that "there was no hesitation at all on my part. . . . I was determined not to give him advice."

The adoption of this policy required, for credibility, both public announcement as well as private observance. At the Montevideo Conference of American States in 1933, Hull made only a slight reservation to a resolution declaring intervention illegal. At the next conference at Buenos Aires in 1936, he made no reservation to a protocol declaring intervention to be "inadmissible"; and at the Lima conference in 1938 he agreed, as previously quoted, that no state had "the right" to intervene in another's domestic or foreign affairs.

From the time the last marines returned from Nicaragua in January 1933, a period of three decades elapsed before armed forces of the United States were again landed on the territory of a Latin American country, breaking a tradition of military nonintervention that had satisfied the most insistent demands made upon the

United States by Latin American countries following the First World War. That tradition had gone far toward eliminating the ill will that had been earlier aroused by policies of dollar diplomacy and "the big stick." The policy was adopted before the threat of Nazi power or the Axis coalition was recognized. It was an American solution to American problems, largely unaffected by considerations of world politics. It did, however, provide a solid basis for Latin American confidence in American policies when, in 1937 and after, the security of the Americas began to be a matter of serious concern in Washington.

The United States as Mediator

In another realm, that of relations among the Latin American countries themselves, the United States also established a reputation for nonintervention in the interwar years. For fifty years after 1881, when Chile defeated Bolivia and Peru in the War of the Pacific, no international conflict had occurred in South America. But in the decade 1932–41, three occasions of warfare between South American countries attracted the sympathy and concern of their sister republics. The United States took an important mediatory role in each of these disputes —not alone, but in concert with other American governments. In so doing, it demonstrated both a deep sense of responsibility for preventing war and restoring peace, and an absolute refusal to employ coercion on behalf of one or other of the contestants. This was the second lesson learned by American politicians during this period: in Latin American wars, do not interfere unilaterally, but try to discover and adopt the most effective procedures for cooperative peace-keeping. This approach later helped shape the methods of peaceful settlement of disputes written into the Charter of the Organization of American States.

The Chaco War between Bolivia and Paraguay, 1932–35, was a bloody conflict in which some 135,000 men were killed. The Bolivians attempted to conquer Paraguay to secure an outlet to the Atlantic Ocean via the Paraguay–La Plata river system. They attacked across the desert and jungle of the Chaco Plain, led by a German general, Hans Kundt. A truce was reached after the Paraguayans drove them back against their mountains. However, it took three more years of peace-keeping efforts by a peace commission of Argentina, Brazil, Peru, Uruguay, and the United States before a treaty was signed in 1938 that described a new and definitive boundary and ratified the military positions at the end of fighting.

In 1932, a group of Peruvian irregulars from Iquitos invaded Colombian territory and occupied the town of Leticia, Colombia's port on the Amazon. Casualties were light, but the Peruvian government supported the

A long-standing boundary dispute between Bolivia and Paraguay erupted in war in 1933. Together with Latin American countries, the United States mediated between the warring sides, leading to an armistice in 1935 and a peace treaty in 1938. Left: Bolivian forces load equipment on to a Junkers transport plane. Below left: Bolivian cavalry pose in front of a tank. Below right: General Hans Kundt, shown inspecting troops, was among several German officers who trained and led Bolivian soldiers.

Museo Storica della Difesa, Asunción/Leigheb

The year the Chaco War began, a group of Peruvians invaded Colombia and seized the port of Leticia. Above: This painting shows war-weary Paraguay soldiers on the march. Left: Leticia, briefly occupied by Peruvian forces, was later returned to Colombia.

invaders. Both countries prepared for war and sent naval forces to Leticia. In this affair the United States took the initiative to remind Peru of its obligation to maintain peace under the Kellogg-Briand Pact. It also assailed the Peruvian government's support for what the United States called "the illegal occupation of Leticia." This charge, bitterly resented in Lima, was rejected by President Sánchez Cerro, and Peruvian cruisers headed for the Panama Canal toward Leticia. Frustrated, Secretary Stimson took no further action, but his successor, Hull, approved the successful participation of the League of Nations in a peace settlement. Following the victory of Colombian forces in the small but critical battle of Tarapacá, and the assassination of Sánchez Cerro, a new Peruvian government agreed to the evacuation of Leticia and Colombia's retention of the port. In these two disputes the Roosevelt administration's efforts to keep the peace were outside the formal agencies of the Pan American Union.

A third conflict erupted in 1941 with an invasion of southwestern Ecuador by the Peruvian army. The United States associated itself informally with Argentina, Brazil, and Chile to restrain the invaders and remove them from the province of Loja. The peace treaty, the Protocol of Rio de Janeiro, was signed on January 29, 1942. The four mediators had persuaded Ecuador to make substantial territorial sacrifices to secure a firm boundary and escape further Peruvian advances. Later Ecuadorian governments were to denounce the protocol on the ground that it was imposed by force of arms. It is clear, however, that in these three instances of international conflict in the Americas, the United States position was one of solicitude and persuasion. It had moved away from the imposition of solutions by economic and military pressures.

Disputes over Oil

By demonstrating in Cuba that it would not intervene in situations of "anarchy," and that it would refrain from coercion in interstate conflicts, the United States, quite apart from considerations arising from world politics, had taken important steps to gain the good will and confidence of its Latin neighbors. However, one further major test had to be passed before hemispheric unity (exclusive of Argentina) was obtained in the Second World War. This test was posed in the late 1930s in three disputes between Latin American governments and United States oil companies. America had already learned two lessons, now it learned another: if the United States forswore intervention, it had to find methods other than force or arbitration to assist its citizens abroad.

In March 1937, the Bolivian government confiscated properties of the Standard Oil Company of Bolivia, alleging that the company had illegally exported oil to Argentina. The government in La Paz, charging fraud in evasion of taxes, asserted that it would pay no compensation. It also refused to submit the question to arbitration, despite a formal proposal by the US Department of State. The dispute dragged on for more than four years. The department failed to induce Bolivia's neighbors to refuse to aid that country in the production and export of oil, but it did bring a negative pressure to bear by refusing to authorize loans to Bolivia by the Export-Import Bank or the Reconstruction Finance Corporation. The issue was finally settled at the Rio de Janeiro conference in 1942 when Bolivia was enabled to make a payment of $1.5 million to the company from a $25 million economic development loan financed by United States agencies. This settlement was facilitated by Washington's fears that German firms might secure oil concessions from Bolivia, and by the revelation in July 1941 of a plot to overthrow the Bolivian government in which the German minister to Bolivia was suspected of being involved. These developments weakened the Department of State's support for arbitration; and after Pearl Harbor the need to have full access to Bolivia's tin helped make easy a settlement negotiated in a few days at Rio de Janeiro.

Mexico's expropriation of American, British, and Dutch oil companies in March 1938 was a far more serious matter. In the first place, the amounts of money involved were far greater—in the order of $400 million according to company claims. And memories of the Pancho Villa incident were still vivid in Mexico. (Two decades earlier the United States had sent a force of 15,000 soldiers into Mexico to try and catch the bandit Villa, who had killed seventeen American civilians in a raid on the town of Columbus, New Mexico.)

President Lázaro Cárdenas was angered by the arrogance of the oil companies in refusing to accept a wage decision of a Mexican labor board. He took a calculated risk that the new Good Neighbor would not intervene on behalf of the oil firms. The Mexican ambassador to the United States, Francisco Castillo Nájera, stated that Mexicans "feared for the fate of the country" at the time. But when an American businessman told him in June 1938 that the United States would intervene, he replied that "Roosevelt would not commit such an attack, both because of his personal sentiments, and because of the international pledge of the Non-Intervention Protocol." (The protocol had been accepted by the United States at the Buenos Aires conference in 1936.)

Washington demanded arbitration of the dispute, which was rejected by Mexico. Consequently, in harmony with the Bolivian case, the Department of State quietly abandoned arbitration as outside the scope of "good neighborly" methods of settlement in expropriation cases. The Mexicans' rejection of arbitration was solidly based:

President Plutarco E. Calles in 1927 had publicly stated that "painful experience" had shown "that arbitration courts adopt the viewpoints of the strong nations, which always dominate." Without acceding to this statement, the Department of State finally accepted Mexico's refusal. Since that time, in comparable cases in the Americas, demands for arbitration have all but disappeared from the repertoire of North American diplomatic pressures.

The situation remained at an impasse for three years. Mexico steadfastly refused to arbitrate and the State Department slowly approved the Mexican proposal for an intergovernmental joint commission to determine the amount of compensation to be paid to the companies. Washington's final action in 1941 was closely linked to a desire to gain the use of air bases in Mexico for refueling of military planes going to and from Panama. Mexico was willing to cooperate in "the common defense," but only on condition that a "general political agreement" was reached. Such agreement had to include the expropriation question. Despite the intransigent opposition of the oil companies, Hull, concerned about the defense of the canal in case of war with Japan, felt, with Roosevelt, that "we could not wait longer." On November 19, 1941, just three weeks before Pearl Harbor, the joint commission of two members was established and arrangements were made for settlement of agrarian claims and provision of credits to Mexico by the Export-Import Bank. In 1943 the joint commission authorized the payment of $23 million to United States oil companies.

This notable victory for Mexican diplomacy was hailed by American Ambassador Josephus Daniels as the "Day of Deliverance." The policy of the United States had been closely watched throughout Latin America. There is little question that Roosevelt and Hull demonstrated the solid evidence of forbearance and moderation that gave reality

to their declarations to refrain from intervention. The completion of the agreement with Mexico before Pearl Harbor gave further strength to the policy of the Good Neighbor.

The new noninterventionist policy, as might have been expected, was soon tested in Venezuela, Latin America's greatest petroleum exporter. If the United States only weakly defended its oil companies against expropriation, what would it do in case of lesser types of restraints on the companies? Venezuela's exports were 90 per cent oil. It did not plan expropriation, but as early as June 1939 its government had appreciated the significance of Washington's policy in Mexico. When one oil company officer protested illegal customs duties on his company's imports, threatening to appeal to the Department of State, a Venezuelan cabinet minister countered the appeal with the reply: "And do you think your government will give you any assistance?"

In fact, the United States gave vital assistance to the companies, but in a very special sense. The Department of State was determined that the expropriation experience in Mexico should not be repeated in Venezuela. It adopted a mature attitude in its relations with US oil companies that is demonstrated in an internal memorandum of June 26, 1939. A remarkable change in policy was spelled out:

. . . this government must be prepared to go further than may be customary in advising the American petroleum companies in the course they should pursue. It must not be permitted them (as occurred in the case of the Mexican dispute) to jeopardize our entire Good Neighbor policy through obstinacy and short-sightedness. Our national interests as a whole far outweigh those of the petroleum companies.

The Department of State thus initiated a campaign of pressure—not on Venezuela, but on Gulf, Standard of

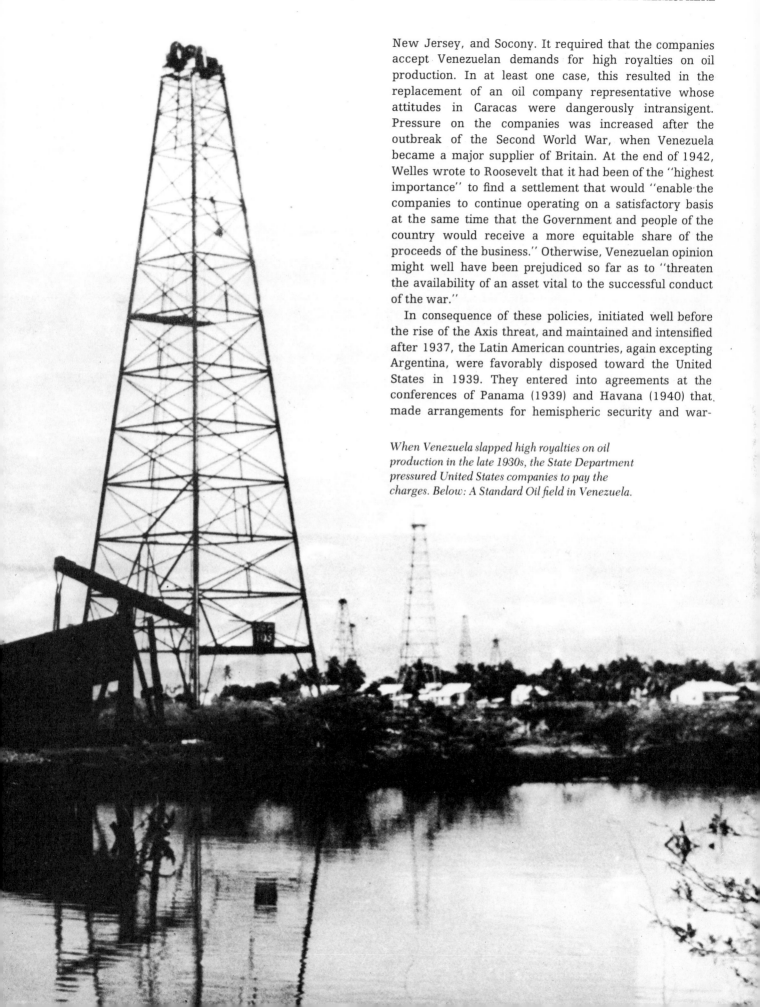

New Jersey, and Socony. It required that the companies accept Venezuelan demands for high royalties on oil production. In at least one case, this resulted in the replacement of an oil company representative whose attitudes in Caracas were dangerously intransigent. Pressure on the companies was increased after the outbreak of the Second World War, when Venezuela became a major supplier of Britain. At the end of 1942, Welles wrote to Roosevelt that it had been of the "highest importance" to find a settlement that would "enable the companies to continue operating on a satisfactory basis at the same time that the Government and people of the country would receive a more equitable share of the proceeds of the business." Otherwise, Venezuelan opinion might well have been prejudiced so far as to "threaten the availability of an asset vital to the successful conduct of the war."

In consequence of these policies, initiated well before the rise of the Axis threat, and maintained and intensified after 1937, the Latin American countries, again excepting Argentina, were favorably disposed toward the United States in 1939. They entered into agreements at the conferences of Panama (1939) and Havana (1940) that made arrangements for hemispheric security and war-

When Venezuela slapped high royalties on oil production in the late 1930s, the State Department pressured United States companies to pay the charges. Below: A Standard Oil field in Venezuela.

time cooperation. Brazil sent troops that made a notable record in Italy, and permitted the United States to establish air bases in her northeast states for the duration. Other countries joined in the cooperative effort to maintain the production of key supplies such as tin and copper.

When Senator Hugh A. Butler of Nebraska launched an attack on the Good Neighbor policy in *Reader's Digest* in 1943, he was denounced by political leaders of both parties in the United States who were buttressed by an outpouring of praise for Roosevelt's policies in the Latin American press. Butler's attack led to a strong expression of satisfaction in Latin America with the transformation of American policy that had begun with Stimson's disillusionment with intervention in Nicaragua.

The Growth of Canadian Identity

The United States did not have to transform its policies toward Canada in order to become a good neighbor. The boundary problems between the countries had been peaceably settled before the First World War, and their water frontiers were regulated by the International Joint Commission formed in 1909. America had not seriously contemplated annexing any part of Canada since at least 1867, and relations between the two countries were bedeviled neither by American interventions nor by Canadian expropriations.

Traditional fears of improbable events lingered on, however. In Canada, it was not until 1931 that "Defence Scheme No. 1," which was based on the view that "the principal external threat to the security of Canada lay in the possibility of armed invasion by the forces of the United States," was officially expunged from the record, and copies in the hands of regional military commanders were burned.

In fact, Canada's relations with the United States in the interwar period were friendly, but formal and distant. Canada's other foreign relations were affected far more by her attendance at the Imperial Conferences of the British Commonwealth and her membership in the League of Nations, than by consultation or cooperation with other American states. Indeed, Ottawa and Washington did not establish direct diplomatic relations until 1927. These relationships had previously been handled by the British embassy. One step in this development was taken by Canada's minister of fisheries, Ernest Lapointe. In 1923, to the surprise of the British ambassador and the Department of State, Lapointe was given authority by the Canadian prime minister to sign alone on behalf of Canada an agreement on fishing rights, known as the Halibut Treaty, which had been negotiated with the United States. This was the first occasion on which an official of the British government had not added his signature

to such a document before it was sent to the Crown for approval.

In this long journey from colony to independent state, important strides had been taken during the First World War. Canadian troops, after a sharp dispute with Lord Kitchener, were commanded by Canadian, not British, officers. Canada, with the other Dominions, was a member of the Imperial War Conference, which by resolution in 1917 asserted "the full recognition of the Dominions as autonomous nations of an imperial commonwealth." Shortly after the war, Canada demonstrated both its influence in the empire's affairs, and, significantly, its deep concern about being placed in a position where, by supporting Britain, Canada might find itself in conflict with fundamental security interests of the United States.

When the Anglo-Japanese Alliance came up for renewal at the Imperial Conference of 1921, Canada alone was opposed, pointing out that it should not be forced to choose between Britain and the United States should the latter become involved in a war with Japan. The alliance was not renewed. Canada remained free from any political or military commitments, either to Britain or the United States.

This was a noteworthy step toward the definition of a Canadian personality in world politics. Ottawa's influence had been potent enough to reverse a major policy of the British Foreign Office. Canada demonstrated a capacity to mediate between the two great English-speaking powers so that their good relations should not be impaired and thus adversely and painfully damage Canadian interests. It also exhibited, as never before, a sense of both dependence and reliance on the power and the policy of the United States. This action may be regarded as the beginning of a slowly maturing relationship, with many hitches and setbacks, that John Bartlet Brebner, a Canadian-American historian, characterized in 1945 by calling the two countries "the Siamese Twins of North America who cannot separate and live."

The determination of Canada and the other Dominions to assert their separate identities and their independence was formally satisfied in 1931 with the passage by the British Parliament of the Statute of Westminster. This measure provided the legal and technical basis for the realization of the status of the Dominions embodied in the Balfour Declaration of the Imperial Conference of 1926: "They are autonomous communities within the British Empire, equal in status, in no way subordinate one to another in any aspect of their domestic or external affairs, though united by a common allegiance to the Crown, and freely associated as members of the British Commonwealth of Nations."

Henceforth, no act of the British Parliament, nor any policy of the British Foreign Office, necessarily had any effect on Canadian law or policy. However, the passage of the statute did not mean that the foreign policies of the two nations would diverge, nor that Canada's would approximate that of the United States. In the League of Nations, Canada voted for the application of sanctions to restrict trade with Italy in the Ethiopian crisis of 1936. Facing the rise of Nazi power in Germany, Canada's government viewed favorably the appeasement policy of Britain through the final phase of the Munich agreement of 1938. In 1937, Prime Minister Mackenzie King had discussions with Adolf Hitler and reported that he was impressed by Hitler's concern for Germany's domestic recovery. He let Hitler know that in case of war, Canada would stand at Britain's side, but he appears to have been convinced at the time that Hitler would not risk a general European conflict. Throughout the 1930s until 1939, Canada's policy was one of noninvolvement in political developments in both Europe and the Far East. Canada did not follow United States policy in passing neutrality legislation. But it also refused, after Munich, to agree to Britain's request that its airmen be trained in Canada and that the two countries begin to stockpile armaments.

Mackenzie King consistently avoided making any commitment as to what Canada might do in case of war. His repeated refrain to all questions was "Parliament will decide." He knew that any expression of intent on his part could only be divisive within Canada.

Relations with Washington in the early 1930s were correct but hardly cordial. In 1928, the United States limited immigration of Canadians to America, nearly stopping a flow that had reached a total of over 1 million during the 1920s. In 1930, the Hawley-Smoot Tariff Act placed higher customs duties on many goods, including some of the principal imports from Canada. In response, Canada raised its own tariff and joined the imperial preference trading system in 1931, in which it gained special, lower duties on its exports to Britain. But this source of ill feeling was largely eliminated by the negotiation of a trade agreement offered in 1934 by the Roosevelt administration.

In the political realm, Ottawa began to realize in the early 1930s that the capacity of Britain to exercise world-wide military power was seriously declining. Consequently, Canada's position would depend more and more on the maintenance of good relations with the United States, and less and less on assistance from London in any dispute or conflict. Thus, Canada's foreign policy aimed both at taking no initiatives that might antagonize the United States and at complying fully with its treaty and other commitments in dealings with Washington.

However, this development did not mean that Canada became anxious to join the inter-American system. Although Roosevelt's Good Neighbor policy was originally intended to apply to the world as a whole, it soon found its almost exclusive response in Latin America. While the growing strength of the ties between Washington and Latin America offered Canada the opportunity to become

a member of the new international alignment in cooperation with the United States, Canada never took a seat in the empty chair available to it at sessions of the Pan American Union. After the failure of the League of Nations to block Italy's annexation of Ethiopia, Canada's isolationist position became more marked than ever. As late as Munich, King appeared to believe that, as a Canadian representative at the league assembly had said in 1924, Canada lived in a "fireproof house far from inflammable materials."

Closer Relations in the Shadow of War

Nevertheless, as the ominous clouds of war became more visible, policy both in Ottawa and Washington began to change, slowly at first, then very rapidly. The change began with a statement by Roosevelt at Chautauqua on August 4, 1936. The United States, he said, could and would "defend itself and defend its neighborhood." Canada did not rush to be certain that she, as well as Mexico, was a neighbor. Shortly afterwards, Roosevelt became more explicit, and again Canada maintained her distance. In a speech in August 1938 at Kingston, Ontario, the president said that "the people of the United States will not stand idly by if domination of Canadian soil is threatened by any other Empire." While this speech was welcomed by many Canadians, Prime Minister King responded rather coolly, saying in effect that Canada did not need United States help. He said that Canada had obligations as a "good, friendly neighbor." One obligation was to see that Canada was made as immune as possible from enemy attack, so that no enemy forces could cross Canadian territory to menace the United States.

This was the public position until the outbreak of the Second World War. Privately, there was one other attempt by Washington to foster hemispheric unity. In September 1937, Roosevelt visited Victoria, British Columbia, and became concerned over the nearly defenseless condition of Canada's Pacific coast. At his invitation, Canadian officers secretly visited Washington on three occasions in 1938 to talk informally about the defense of Puget Sound and Vancouver Island. These talks were discontinued, however, after November 1938 and were not renewed until the summer of 1940. Earlier, in 1936, the Canadian government had rejected an American proposal for the construction of what later came to be the Alcan or Alaska highway. Before the outbreak of the Second World War, therefore, the United States pursued hemispheric unity in a mild fashion. And Canada, disagreeing with Washington's view that danger was imminent, was wary of commitments and insistent on total autonomy in policy. Mackenzie King in the summer of 1938 asserted that the existing danger of attack on

Canada "is minor in degree and second-hand in origin."

The outbreak of war in 1939 brought a dramatic and enduring change in American-Canadian relationships. Canada's Parliament almost unanimously gave its approval to a declaration of war on the Axis powers a week after Great Britain. Canada did not opt for neutrality as had the United States, nor did Canada request any assurances from Washington. Despite its prior no-commitment posture, a commitment to Britain and France was almost immediately assumed. Basic elements

Following the outbreak of war, Canada reversed its former role and pursued hemispheric unity. It did not join the Pan American Union, but it began to seek both arms for itself and various types of economic and military aid for its European allies. Now it was the turn of the United States to resist advances. Hampered by political opposition, the neutrality legislation, and by a shortage of war materials in 1939, Roosevelt did not respond affirmatively until the position of Britain became desperate after the fall of France in June 1940. Then, swiftly,

New York Daily News

Opposite: America was neutral during the Ethiopian crisis, but Canada supported sanctions against Italy. This Fortune *cartoon appeared before the League of Nations failed to halt Italy's invasion. Its legend read: "Half a league, half a league, half a league onward!" Above: Hitler's actions alarmed the United States more than Canada. This mid-1939 photo shows the Roosevelts being visited by British royalty and the Canadian prime minister. To the right of Queen Elizabeth are King George VI, FDR, James, Sara, and Eleanor Roosevelt, and Prime Minister Mackenzie King.*

here were the latent, deep-rooted ties of the majority of Canadians to the mother countries—Britain and France. There was an equally deep feeling by the great majority of Canadians that this action was an affirmation of Canadian nationality, separate and distinct from what many regarded as "the encroaching culture" of America.

cooperation became intimate, effective, and generally successful.

The critical decisions were taken, this time at Roosevelt's invitation, at a meeting with Mackenzie King at Ogdensburg, New York, in August 1940. King was informed of the agreement to exchange fifty American destroyers for long leases on British bases in the Western Hemisphere, including Newfoundland, which was not then a member of the Canadian confederation. King did not protest the plan, and later Canada accepted seven of the destroyers to aid in protecting convoys. Of greater importance, however, was King's immediate acceptance, without consultation with Parliament, of Roosevelt's proposal for the appointment of a Permanent Joint Board on Defense. As one historian summed up the relations of these two great democracies: "More than ever each people realizes that its independence and liberty depend on the independence and liberty of the other."

Chapter 3

FIREBELL IN THE EAST

Stability in the Far East was dashed soon after the First World War. The region's strongest power, Japan, quickly fell under the control of military leaders determined to extend their influence into Chinese territory. At the same time, China was in the midst of a nationalist revolution aimed at uniting its sprawling dominions. But the ruling party of Chiang Kai-shek was riddled with corruption and dissent, and the Japanese were soon acting in defiance of the peace treaties they had pledged to uphold. Washington reacted to Japanese aggression with sharp condemnation— but little else. No president could have undertaken military action in a region where events, for most Americans, seemed to pose little threat to national security.

Japan Resorts to Force

For American interests in the Far East, the First World War was catastrophic. Those interests—the security of the Philippine Islands and the maintenance of the principles of the Open Door in China—required a power balance in the area, but that balance had been upset by Japan. Under cover of the war, the Japanese had taken over Germany's holdings in Shantung and her islands in the northern Pacific. They had also wrested substantial and extensive concessions from China as a result of twenty-one demands made in 1915. And, as a consequence of taking part in an Allied expedition against the Bolsheviks in 1918, their troops were lodged in eastern Siberia and in the northern half of Sakhalin Island. Efforts by President Wilson at the peace conference to restore the balance by depriving Japan of her wartime gains proved fruitless. The end of the war found Japan in a preponderant position in eastern Asia. No wonder that a first order of diplomatic business in the new Harding administration was, to use the words of John V. A. MacMurray, chief of the State Department Far Eastern Division, to restore "the equilibrium in the Far East which had been so dangerously upset by Japan's process of aggrandizement."

The opportunity arose at the conference in Washington, called by the United States in November of 1921, to consider the limitation of naval armament. Although the Senate approved the Washington treaties handily in March of 1922, many observers were concerned that, given Japan's strengthened position and the absence of enforcement machinery in the arrangements, American security, in the final analysis, rested on Japan's good will. Indeed, as they viewed the situation in the Far East, they concluded that the only constraint upon Japan's conduct was her willingness to honor the commitments and pledges made in the treaties.

Administration leaders, however, were not alarmed. They were convinced of Japan's good will and intent to abide by the treaties. As MacMurray wrote in 1924, the Japanese were "a friendly people who have shown themselves disposed to put aside mutual distrust and rivalry to co-operate loyally with us in our traditional Far Eastern policies." All the evidence pointed to the fact that, having received security for the homeland and fair treatment at Washington, the Japanese had abandoned their aggressive designs in favor of conciliation toward China.

The drift of Japanese political and social development gave additional promise of a peaceful and cooperative program. Great steps were being taken in establishing a liberal, democratic, Western-style parliamentary system. Cabinet government and party responsibility were instituted and the suffrage was extended to all males. Military budgets were cut and social reforms were begun. The political leadership of the country supported disarmament, membership in the League of Nations, and the peaceful settlement of disputes. Typical was Kijuro Shidehara, the foreign minister—liberal, antimilitarist, Western-oriented (he wrote his state papers in English)—who could be depended upon to direct Japan's foreign policy with "the most scrupulous regard for its honor and the fulfillment of its commitments," to use the words of historian James T. Shotwell.

Encouraging, too, was the apparent inclination of the majority of the Japanese people to support the liberals and the civilian element in their country as against the military clique, which was the exponent of a unilateral and warlike policy on the Asian mainland and of imperialism and expansion. As one observer noted, "the Japanese military have not, by any means been silenced. But their voices are no longer the voices of Japan. Their ultranationalism is being tempered by contacts with a new Japan that feels itself part of a world-wide movement to end war, to remedy economic injustice, to establish for the good of the common man the institution of democracy." There was every reason to believe that the rule of those responsible for the twenty-one demands had been replaced by the rule of those responsible for ratifying the Washington treaties.

Important, too, was the position of the Japanese business community. It stood solidly behind the government's policy of peace and conciliation. Its close financial and commercial connection with the United States provided a virtual guarantee that it would not support a reckless and warlike course in Asia. It could hardly afford to alienate or affront the country which took 40 per cent of Japan's exports, which provided more of Japan's imports than any other country, and which supplied large amounts of capital to Japanese industries and municipalities.

Administration leaders could point, as well, to conditions in China as an augury for stability in the Far East and for the maintenance of the new order. That populous and sprawling country was in the midst of a nationalist revolution guided by Sun Yat-sen, father of the republic, and his lieutenant, Chiang Kai-shek, as leaders of the Kuomintang or Nationalist party. A new leadership, which had emerged during the war and consisted of young, foreign-educated intellectuals, was dedicated to strengthening China and ridding her of foreign control. Measures were being taken to modernize the government and to effect social, financial, and judicial reforms.

When Sun died in 1925, Chiang took over the direction of the revolution and undertook a drive to unify the country by unseating the war lords who ruled as independent chieftains each in his own area. By the end of 1926, the southern half of the country had come under Chiang's control. In the same year, the Northern Expedition was launched, leading to the occupation of Nanking in March of 1927, where the capital of the "new China" was estab-

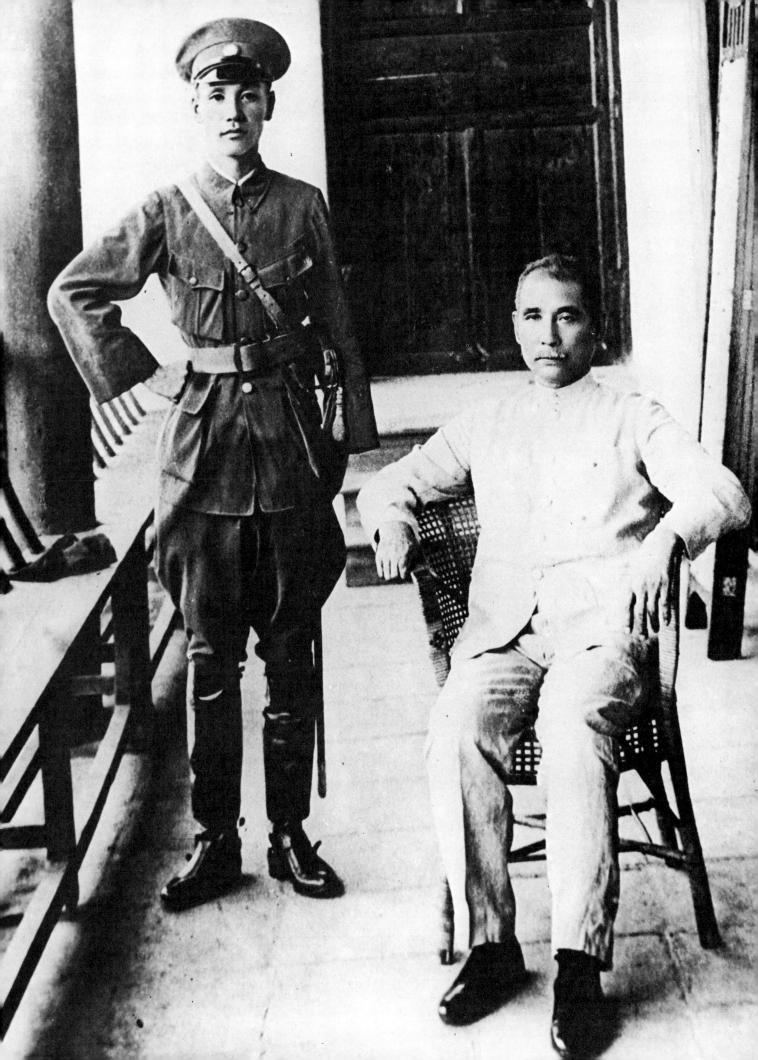

lished, and of Peking in June of the next year. At Sun's temporary grave in that city, Chiang reported to the "father of the nation" that his dream had been achieved.

At the same time, Chiang was continuing Sun's program of ending the special rights foreigners had enjoyed for more than a century and which had kept China in a weakened and subservient position. Of importance was Chiang's break with the Soviet Union in 1927 after years of close collaboration. That country had played an important role in the movement to unify China. In 1924, a formal Soviet-Chinese alliance was consummated and, thereafter, all sorts of help came from Moscow. Communists, Chinese as well as Russian, were taken into important positions in the government and there was a good deal of concern in the West at the prospect of China coming under Red influence. No wonder the break was greeted with relief. Much was made of China's new-found unity, stability, and independence as factors in enabling Chiang and his government to maintain the principles of the Open Door and to keep the Japanese at bay.

Sources of Instability

Unhappily for America's position in the Far East, the roseate estimate of the situation made by the defenders of the Washington settlement proved inaccurate. China never did (at least until 1949) achieve sufficient strength or stability to play the role envisaged by Americans. She was continually troubled by civil strife and internal disorders and by venality and corruption in the rank and file of government officials. The unity achieved by Chiang was more apparent than real. A true central government did not exist. War lords remained powerful in their areas and Chiang's Nationalist regime in Nanking could not speak for the whole nation in dealing with foreigners in China or in international negotiations. In large parts of the country, chaos prevailed and many people wondered whether order could ever be achieved. Bandits were commonplace and Nanking seemed incapable of protecting life and property. Such a condition was a sure invitation to intervention by foreign governments on behalf of their nationals.

Most observers attributed China's problems to the quality of leadership and to dissension in the ruling Nationalist party—the Kuomintang. It was split between left and right elements, and friction existed not only between the two wings but within each. As to the chief figures in the party, MacMurray could find no "element of

Sun Yat-sen (seated) and Chiang Kai-shek spearheaded the drive to make China a united, independent republic free of foreign control. When Sun died in 1925, Chiang took over as China's leader.

purpose and of patriotic idealism . . . in the vast complex of self-seeking jealousy and intrigue into which the movement has disintegrated . . . outside of the self-interest of certain militarists who have grouped themselves together for their own common profit." And Chiang, the supreme leader, he found "most untrustworthy." Such views were echoed by other China specialists in the State Department, such as Nelson T. Johnson, who served in the 1920s as chief of the Far Eastern Division of the department and minister to China, and Ferdinand Meyer, a career foreign service officer with long experience in China.

As for Japan, American policy-makers had made as serious a miscalculation as they had concerning China. They had enormously underestimated the determination and resolve of the military clique to capture the government and to embark upon a course of expansion and conquest on the mainland. To a passionately patriotic group of young officers, the Washington settlement was "the lost rights conference." There, they claimed, Japan had been relegated to a lesser position as indicated by the unequal tonnage ratios. They ignored Article Nineteen (a pledge by the United States and Britain not to add to existing fortifications, or erect new ones, in any of their island possessions in the Pacific save Hawaii and the small islands off the coasts of Canada, New Zealand, and Australia) which more than made up for the smaller figure. Instead they pointed to the weakened position in which the fleet was placed.

But it was not only getting the short end which angered them: their country had been humiliated and treated as an inferior state. It was characteristic, they insisted, of the attitude of Caucasians toward Asians. They appealed to their countrymen to renounce the liberal civilian government's policy of conciliation with the West in favor of a program of unilateral military action. The Caucasians, they said, could never willingly permit Japan to enjoy her fair share of the land and resources of Asia, hence that share must be taken by force. The government had betrayed the people; only the military could save them.

Of all the Western powers who threatened Japanese honor and security, it was the United States which stood preeminent in the eyes of the military. They had always regarded the nation on the other side of the Pacific as the obstacle which stood in the path of Japanese advance and which, someday, would have to be fought and defeated if Japan's destiny in Asia were to be realized. And they had evidence enough to support the view.

It was true that the United States had acquiesced tacitly in Japan's claim to a privileged position in Manchuria, Mongolia, and certain parts of China in the decade and a half before the outbreak of the First World War. But it was also true that it was the United States which alone had challenged Japan's twenty-one demands upon China in 1915 in the form of a "caveat." Worse, it was President Wilson who at the end of the war had sought to deprive Japan of Shantung, to revive an old scheme for an international consortium to lend money to China which would have weakened Japan's position on the mainland, and to claim cable rights on the Japanese-mandated island of Yap. It was Wilson, too, who had dealt the final blow at the peace conference to Japan's demand that a racial equality clause be included in the League of Nations Covenant. And when the Allies sent troops into Siberia in 1918, it was clear that the chief mission of the American contingent was to monitor the Japanese forces and check any Japanese plans to gain a foothold in Soviet territory.

Of all the evidence of American hostility, the most damning was racial discrimination. There had been for many years, and particularly in the western states, a movement to restrict the movement of Japanese, to prohibit them from owning land, and to keep them from entering the country. The agitation led to the passage in 1920 of laws in several states denying the Japanese the right to own or rent land, and to a federal statute in 1924 excluding them from migrating to America. The affront to the Japanese people was incalculable, particularly the exclusion act. News of the legislation was received with shock in Japan. The day the law went into effect was pro-

claimed National Humiliation Day and fifteen Tokyo newspapers printed a joint declaration condemning it. Demonstrations against the United States broke out all over Japan. That the measure strengthened the hands of the military and discredited the liberals was indisputable. An official of the Japanese embassy in Washington warned that the law would spell death to the party of conciliation.

The law was a needless insult to a proud people. If only Japan had been assigned a quota of immigrants as other nations had received in the Immigration Act of 1921, no more than 250 Japanese would have entered the country in any one year. The price paid for singling them out as undesirable was very great, and many important Americans feared the consequences. Secretary of State Charles Evans Hughes, who had done his best to block the law, wrote: "It is a sorry business and I am greatly depressed. It has undone the work of the Washington

The United States ban on Japanese immigration infuriated Japan, which viewed the move as a hostile, racist act. This is how the Japan Times *reported the demonstrations that followed.*

ANTI-AMERICA DAY OBSERVED BY ALL JAPAN

Tokyo Ablaze With Fire Of Roused Nation's Patriotism

LEADERS URGING CALM PROTESTS

Throngs Jam Shrine During Day; America Called Danger To Peace

Today is Anti-America Day in Japan. The Capital is plastered with signs and fluttering with flags that enjoin the populace to calm and sober protest against the insulting action of the American Congress in passing the Immigration with its Exclusion clause.

Aroused students and professional men have littered the city with handbills, all of the general tone urging loyal Japanese to observe July 1 as a day of formal objection to such race discrimination.

All through the excitement,

Anti-Exclusion Demonstrators

A few of the very many thousands in Tokyo who voiced their protest against the coming into force of the American Exclusion Act today. This group, carrying a banner which exhorts all to "Raise the National Voice," was snapped in front of the Tokyo Station.

The military increasingly charted the course of Japanese policy in the 1920s. Here, the emperor inspects what look like gigantic sousaphones but were, in fact, air-raid warning devices.

Conference and implanted the seeds of an antagonism which are sure to bear fruit in the future. . . . Our friends in the Senate have in a few minutes spoiled the work of years and done a lasting injury to [the] country.''

There was talk of war between the two countries and a spate of articles appeared in the United States bearing such titles as ''The Menace of Japan'' and ''Must We Fight Japan.'' It was no secret that American naval planners considered Japan the enemy, and a Pacific war inevitable. In making preparations for the conference to limit those classes of warships not considered at Washington, which President Coolidge called to meet in Geneva in 1927, they based their estimates on a war in that ocean. Refining and improving ''Plan Orange''—the strategy, tactics, and logistics of a war with Japan—was the principal preoccupation of American naval staff officers as the 1920s closed.

From 1921, the military in Japan had been on alert for an opportunity to overthrow the civilian government and begin operations on the mainland. Organized into numerous secret societies and study groups, the officer class plotted and planned and waited for the propitious moment to strike. Constitutionally, the army was in a favored position. It was independent of the war minister and of the cabinet, having direct access to the emperor. A coup planned for 1923 was frustrated by a devastating earthquake (whose victims were aided generously by American charity). Four years later, the liberal government fell as a consequence of its failure to punish a Chinese attack on the consulate in Nanking. The new cabinet was headed by

General Giichi Tanaka, a leader of the military clique, a frank advocate of the use of force in achieving Japan's aims in Asia, and reputed author of a blueprint, the Tanaka Memorial, for the conquest and exploitation of China. He unabashedly called for ''a great renovation in our China policy in order to carry out the defense of our country and the protection of our rights.''

A clash between advancing Chinese troops of Chiang Kai-shek's Northern Expedition and Japanese soldiers protecting Japanese nationals in Shantung in May of 1928 may have signaled the beginning of ''drastic action,'' but the incident went no further than a few encounters. There was too much opposition to an aggressive policy by the emperor, important liberals and civilians, and the business interests who feared desperately a disruption of trade with China in the event of war. Tanaka was forced to resign in 1929 after the murder of Chang Tso-lin, the Chinese war lord in Manchuria, by officers of the Kwantung army whom Tanaka failed to punish. He was succeeded by Yuro Hamaguchi, a moderate civilian, as premier, and Shidehara once again became foreign minister.

There seems to be no question that the army was becoming more and more restless and eager to move on the mainland. The attack on the life of Premier Hamaguchi in November of 1930 (resulting in his death six months later) by some jingo officers was an indication of the state of the army and a harbinger of coming events. Indeed, 1930 seems to have been a turning point as far as the determination of the army to embark upon a policy of conquest was concerned. A series of incidents on the mainland in the summer of 1931—a Chinese attack on some Koreans near Changchun; the disappearance under mysterious circumstances of a Japanese army major whose body, dressed in civilian clothes, was found in the vicinity of Harbin and whose death was laid to Chinese soldiers; a growing and damaging boycott in many major Chinese cities of Japanese goods—gave the military ample pretext and a feeling of confidence that a punitive expedition against the Chinese would receive wide popular support.

Most significant in the catalogue of factors propelling the army to action was the increasing effort by the Nationalist government to tighten the hold on Manchuria and to unite it with China. As soon as Chiang had succeeded in taking Peking in 1928, he turned his attention to Manchuria. He formed an alliance with Chang Tso-lin, the war lord there, and when he died, gained the allegiance of his son and successor, Chang Hsueh-liang. At the same time, he launched a movement to rid Manchuria of the two powers—Russia and Japan—which had so dominant a position in the area, and to increase the Chinese presence. He began the construction of a port on the opposite side of the Gulf of Pechihli from Dairen to rival that Japanese-held facility, made plans to build a competitive railway line parallel to the South Manchurian, and encouraged Chinese to immigrate and to take up permanent residence. Indeed, by 1931, of the 30 million inhabitants of Manchuria, all but 2 million were Chinese.

Such a program the Japanese could not suffer, for Manchuria had very special relationships with the island empire. For one thing, it was viewed as their "lifeline." Japan's "right of survival" demanded that Manchuria be Japanese, for only that vast and rich region could serve as the outlet for the excess population of the homeland and provide the resources which Japan lacked.

Moreover, Japan possessed extensive rights and interests in the region as a result of several treaties with China and of years of exploitation—two major rail nets (the South Manchurian from Port Arthur and Dairen at the tip of the Liaotung Peninsula to Changchun 400 miles to the north, and the Mukden-Antung line connecting the South Manchurian to the Korean rail system), coal and iron mines, hotels, farms, factories, lumber mills, harbor facilities, and utilities—an investment of over $1 billion. A sizable body of regular troops, the Kwantung army, was garrisoned there and special military guards were stationed along the railroad right of way (one every fifteen kilometers). Not to be underestimated was an invisible connection with Manchuria, a deeply spiritual and emotional link, rooted in the heroic sacrifice of the mikado's soldiers in the war against Russia a quarter of a century earlier. The soil on which so much blood was shed was considered sacred and peculiarly Japanese.

Although the army had plans to make Manchuria a Japanese protectorate as early as 1927 (as reported to Washington by Myrl S. Myers, the American consul-general in Mukden in November of that year), the propitious moment did not come until 1931. Coupled with the events mentioned above were two other factors which made that year crucial. One was the discontent in naval circles in Japan with the results of the naval disarmament conference held in London the previous year. Another was the deepening of the worldwide depression which had begun in 1929. The economic dislocation in Japan created a substantial group of dissatisfied people who looked to the army and to forceful action as the solution for their miseries. The army, in turn, capitalized on the situation promising a "national renovation" to relieve the distress, thereby gaining the mass support which it needed for any adventure on the mainland. In another way

The epitome of military discipline, General Ueda (above) commanded Japan's Manchuria forces. When China tried to strengthen her hold on the area, she met fierce opposition. Among Japanese interests was the South Manchuria railway. The poster at right indicates the extent of the system.

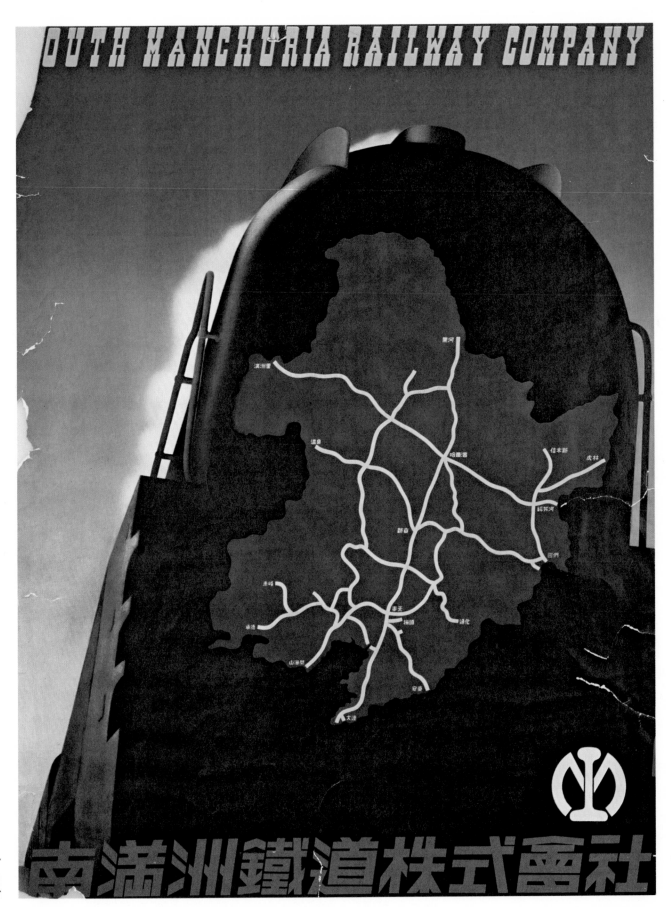

the depression played into the army's hands. It was believed to have so paralyzed the Western powers as to reduce their ability to resist a Japanese advance.

The expected blow came that year, in September. On the eighteenth of that month at 10:00 PM, an explosion on a section of the track of the South Manchuria railway some three miles south of Mukden brought out the Japanese railway guards and soldiers from the Kwantung army. Putting the blame on the Chinese for the incident, they promptly occupied Mukden and within four days had taken control of large parts of southern Manchuria.

To resist the well-trained and tightly disciplined Japanese soldiers would have been folly for Chinese troops. China's only hope to stave off a Japanese conquest lay in calling on the Western powers who had signed the three international agreements which China claimed Japan had violated: the Nine-Power Treaty guaranteeing China's territorial integrity; the 1928 Kellogg-Briand Pact outlawing war as an instrument of national policy; and the League of Nations Covenant Article Ten which guaranteed the independence and integrity of the member states. So on September 21 the call for help went to the League of Nations at Geneva. At the same time, because the United States was not a league member, a separate appeal was sent to Washington.

If China had any hopes of assistance from either source, they were soon dashed. The league council shrank from the challenge to make the Manchurian incident a test of the postwar treaty structure. The risk of war was too great. Hence, the assurance by the Japanese delegate that his country's action was a measure of self-defense to protect the railway (permitted under the Kellogg-Briand Pact) and not an aggressive war designed to impair China's integrity or independence (thus no violation of the Nine-Power Treaty or Article Ten) was accepted with relief. The representatives of the other powers seemed satisfied with Japan's promise to cease operations and withdraw to its proper zone as soon as the situation returned to normal. The council satisfied itself with a resolution on

An explosion on the South Manchuria railway line near Mukden sparked hostilities between Japan and China. This photograph shows Japanese soldiers entering Manchuria shortly after the incident.

Keystone

September 30 expressing confidence in the Japanese explanation.

Washington's reaction was much like the league's. Secretary of State Henry L. Stimson also accepted the Japanese view of the situation. Foreign Minister Shidehara told him that the army had moved on its own without approval of the civilian authorities in Tokyo and, given time, the civilians would reassert their authority and curb the military. But, he warned, time and patience were essential. Precipitate action by the United States would provoke public support for the military and make more difficult the task of the civilians. So Stimson did nothing to embarrass the Japanese Foreign Office.

Although he privately expressed his concern over the Japanese advance and over the fact that the treaties may have been violated, he publicly played no favorites. "We have not attempted to go into the question of right and wrong. . . . We are not taking sides," he said. To both China and Japan he expressed the hope that military operations would soon cease. And to make certain there would be no blame assessed for the event, he discouraged a move by the league council to send a commission of inquiry to Manchuria, which the Chinese favored and the Japanese opposed. As a demonstration of his confidence that the incident would soon be resolved, he permitted the American ambassador in Tokyo to go home on leave.

Whatever the merits of Stimson's policy toward the crisis, there was not much else he could have done. The American people would never have tolerated a tough approach to Japan. They would never have approved running the risk of hostilities for a piece of remote territory in distant Asia, even in support of a principle. Much as they sympathized with the Chinese and castigated the Japanese for their brutal attacks, they had no wish to become involved. Their experience in the world war had taught them the futility of interfering in other nations' struggles.

But even had there been a desire to take sides and help the beleagured Chinese, the state of the military establishment would have made that course impossible. The depression had forced a drastic reduction in the army and navy budgets. Enlisted strength had dropped to dangerous lows, one-third of the fleet was out of service, and the Asiatic squadron had only one heavy cruiser afloat. Further, the absence of strong and well-equipped bases in the Pacific diminished the effective deployment of the fleet, whose base was in San Diego.

Stimson continued to follow a policy of caution, moderation, and patience even when, in October, Japanese aircraft bombed Chinchow, the headquarters of Marshal Chang Hsueh-liang after he left Mukden, and far away from the Japanese railway zone. He was upset and troubled. There appeared no justification for the enlargement of the military operation. Either Shidehara had failed to control the army or he was in collusion with the

jingos. To his diary Stimson confided his determination "to take a firm ground and aggressive stand against Japan." When the league council met on October 13, he instructed the American consul in Geneva, Prentiss Gilbert, to join in its deliberations. When, however, the council approved a resolution demanding that Japan evacuate Chinese territory and withdraw to the railway zone by November 16, Stimson withdrew Gilbert. He feared the effect on Japan of an ultimatum and did not want to be associated with it. He wished to "leave a ladder by which Japan could climb down." He was still willing to give Shidehara time to bridle the military and still unwilling to sit in judgment on Japan. Reluctant to give the appearance of a sharp break with the league, Stimson sent Tokyo a note demanding an evacuation of Chinese territory but, significantly, without setting a deadline date.

November 16 came and went but there was no Japanese withdrawal. Quite the reverse. The Japanese army, on November 3, launched a large-scale attack using infantry, artillery, cavalry, and aircraft on Tsitsihar, a city north of the Chinese Eastern railway and remote from Japan's treaty zone. On the nineteenth, the city was occupied. Less than one month later, on December 11, the liberal Wakatsuki ministry fell, to be replaced by a frankly promilitary government. The forces in Manchuria continued their advance. On January 3, 1932, Chinchow, the last Chinese stronghold in Manchuria, was taken. The beaten and broken Chinese army fled south of the Great Wall. Organized resistance in Manchuria had come to an end.

America's Ineffectual Response

The secretary now felt betrayed. All the promises and pledges on which he had based his policy of "playing no favorites" had proved a hoax. The Japanese people seemed to be solidly behind the "brave soldiers" fighting for the emperor. The moderates were helpless to halt the military. Stimson was not now even sure they wanted to put a brake on the army. They may have been infected with the virus of patriotism and nationalism as were the extremists. He was determined to take strong and positive action against Japan.

The league council had met in Paris on November 16 and Stimson had instructed the American ambassador in London, Charles G. Dawes, to cross the Channel to be available for consultation by the Japanese and Chinese delegates. He was not to take part in the meetings (Gilbert's participation in October had been severely criticized by those in the United States who opposed any American involvement with the league), but it was hoped that his presence would be useful in arriving at a formula to stop the fighting. But neither Dawes nor the council could affect the Japanese determination to dominate Manchuria. When the mikado's representative suggested the appointment of a commission of inquiry to investigate the September incident, the council had to content itself with the action. It had discussed more serious measures, such as economic sanctions, but, in the end, the danger inherent in so drastic a step caused delegates to retreat.

Stimson supported the idea of an inquiry, but he was determined to do something more. Several possibilities existed. Force, or even measures "short of force" such as economic sanctions or an embargo on war materials, was out of the question. He could have demonstrated American displeasure by recalling the ambassador from Tokyo. He could also have convened a conference of the signatories of the Nine-Power Treaty, which would have signaled a presumption that Japan had violated that pact. He did neither but chose, instead, another course—one which had a precedent in American history.

It was popularly called nonrecognition and had been used by Secretary of State William Jennings Bryan seventeen years earlier as a solution to a similar problem. In identical notes to China and to Japan sent on January 7, 1932, Stimson informed the two nations that the United States "cannot admit the legality of any situation *de facto* nor does it intend to recognize any treaty or agreement entered into between those Governments [China and Japan], or agents thereof, which may impair the treaty rights of the United States or its citizens in China. . . . And that it does not intend to recognize any situation, treaty or agreement which may be brought about by means contrary to the . . . Pact of Paris." Although addressed to both nations, the admonition was meant only for Japan. That power alone was upsetting the status quo in eastern Asia.

So Secretary Stimson reproached Japan and conveyed his country's displeasure and disapproval. The action was warmly applauded at home. It was hailed as a welcome expression of American revulsion to Japanese aggression and as a means of strengthening the treaty structure. That it was ineffectual was noted by only a few people, but they were right. It had no effect on Japan's course in Manchuria. Worse still, it actually worsened relations with Japan. Of all the powers, only the United States had censured the island empire's advance on the mainland. Neither Britain nor France had joined Stimson. Indeed, both nations were sympathetic to Japan and did not conceal their approval of the role she played in bringing some semblance of order and stability to China. She was seen not only as a civilizing agent but as a bulwark against the advance of Soviet communism in Asia. The United States did not even gain China's gratitude. The warning to Japan was seen as having the "head of a dragon and the tail of a rat," a scrap of paper, useless without a string of battleships in its wake.

Unafraid and undeterred, the Japanese continued to fasten their hold on Manchuria and to integrate it politically and economically into the empire. Banks, mines, and industries came under Japanese management; purchases from foreign firms were prohibited; business was diverted to Japanese companies; and Japanese served either as advisers to the Chinese administration or themselves occupied posts in the government. The transition to the next step was inevitable—severing Manchuria from China and tying it to Japan. An independence movement, fostered by Kwantung army officers among the Chinese inhabitants, culminated on February 18, 1932 in the proclamation of the new state of Manchukuo with the last of the Manchu emperors, Hsuan-tsung, who had been living in retirement in Tientsin, as ruler.

Now the facade was finally and definitely stripped from Japanese policy. What Japan's statesmen had called a temporary police action to safeguard rights was now revealed as a war to conquer part of China. A large-scale aerial and ground attack against Shanghai in January, launched ostensibly to punish the Chinese for an anti-Japanese boycott and to protect Japanese merchants, gave further evidence of Japan's aggressive designs on the mainland.

International Maneuvers

In the United States there was a growing hostility toward Japan. Manchukuo and Shanghai were viewed as outrageous and immoral acts. It was clear that the Japanese had destroyed the treaty structure so laboriously constructed at Washington in 1921–22 and at Paris in 1928. China's territorial integrity had been violated, the Open Door was closed, and an offensive war had been fought. There was anger and exasperation in Washington and in the rest of the country. Stimson and other policy-makers searched for a means of making known their displeasure and curbing Japan's expansion.

President Herbert Hoover promptly ruled out military action. Neither obligations to China nor American dignity warranted fighting, he said. The controversy was between China and Japan, and the United States had no responsibility for preserving peace and order in the world. Some church groups and peace societies proposed an embargo on exports and loans to Japan, but the administration rejected the idea as too provocative. The president did approve a strong protest to Japan on Shanghai and the dispatch to that port of a cruiser and six destroyers, an infantry regiment, and 400 marines. Stimson's motive in sending military and naval forces was to keep Japan guessing and worried about the possibility of American intervention. He put, he said, great reliance upon "the unconscious element of our great size and military strength. . . . Japan was afraid of that, and I was willing to let her be afraid of that without telling her that we are not going to use it against her.''

His real trump card, however, was to warn Japan sternly that no one signatory could unilaterally abrogate the Nine-Power Treaty without serious consequences. Such a move, however, he did not wish to take alone. He did not wish to repeat the unilateral action of January 7 and bear the brunt of a challenge without support from another power. Britain was, of course, the logical collaborator, but overtures to London were rebuffed. The British government had no wish to cause trouble for Japan. It looked to Japan to defend British interests in Asia. Indeed, it regretted the end of the Anglo-Japanese Alliance. The United States it considered a weak reed.

What was the secretary of state to do? How might he register the repugnance of the American people and

Japan carried out a punitive raid on the Chinese port of Shanghai in 1932. Here, American infantrymen erect barricades in the foreign quarter of the city.

government to Japan's action without a direct protest? The device used was a letter to Senator William E. Borah, powerful chairman of the Senate Foreign Relations Committee, written on February 24, 1932. In it, the secretary reaffirmed American belief in the wisdom and efficacy of the Open Door principle and of the network of treaties signed at Washington in 1922. He appealed to all governments to withhold recognition of any situation arising from a violation of the treaties. Finally, and ominously, there was the threat that the modification or violation of any part of the treaty structure released the United States from any or all of its obligations under the treaties. The implication was unmistakable—the United States would feel free to build capital ships beyond the treaty limitation and strengthen the Pacific bases forbidden by Article Nineteen.

The possibility of American refortification and rearmament caused considerable concern in Tokyo. Additional capital ships and the erection of powerful bastions in Guam and the Philippines posed a grave menace to Japan's dream of hegemony in eastern Asia and the

Keystone

western Pacific. But it did not, for even a moment, change the island empire's course. When the League of Nations assembly, on March 11, 1932, voted to withhold recognition of Manchukuo the Japanese were hardly ruffled. Nor did they permit the report of the league commission of inquiry, submitted on September 4, 1932, to deter them from their determination to dominate the mainland. The commission concluded that the Japanese did not act in self-defense on the night of September 18, 1931, nor was the creation of Manchukuo the consequence of a "genuine and spontaneous independence movement." Still, it did not advocate a return to the pre-September 18 situation. It recommended, instead, as a means of reconciling Japan's rights and China's sovereignty, the election of a special administration for Manchuria under Chinese sovereignty but autonomous. A *gendarmerie*, replacing troops of both nations, would keep order and monitor a proposed Sino-Japanese treaty.

The commission's proposed solution to the problem of Manchuria seemed reasonable to all the powers save Japan. Japan had no intention of sharing Manchuria with China. On September 15, the eve of the report's publication, Tokyo recognized Manchukuo and signed a treaty with the new state which assigned the island empire great and exclusive rights. Five months later, when the league assembly accepted the report, Japan did the expected—gave the league the two year notice of intent to quit the international organization. So the rulers in Tokyo removed themselves from the strictures and censures of world opinion and restraints.

It was now May of 1933. Two months earlier, a new administration had taken over in Washington when Franklin D. Roosevelt replaced Herbert Hoover. But the replacement of Republicans by Democrats did not change America's Far Eastern policy. Both the new president and his secretary of state, Cordell Hull, agreed to continue the Hoover-Stimson doctrine of nonrecognition. Both were prepared to accept the fait accompli in Manchuria. Nor did they protest when Japanese forces, in the spring of 1933, pushed westward into Jehol and southward across the Great Wall into Hopei. Elements of the Japanese army continued on to within thirteen miles of Peking, which the world expected to fall to the emperor's troops. Instead, a Sino-Japanese truce was arranged on May 31, and the fighting stopped. The Japanese, it appeared, were not quite ready to take on China, but they left little doubt that such a course was in the future. A Foreign Office spokesman, Eiji Amau, made it plain in a bellicose statement in April of 1934. He announced that the destiny of East Asia lay in Japan's hands, proclaimed Japanese control of China's relations with the West, and defied the world to interfere in Asian matters.

Washington took no action on that brazen pronouncement. Yet Hull, like Stimson, believed that the policy of the United States ought to be "maintaining the independence of China and in preventing Japan from gaining overlordship of the entire Far East." When the Japanese ambassador in Washington in May of 1934 sought to gain an admission by Hull of Japan's predominant position in East Asia, he was rebuffed. But to resist the Japanese advance was out of the question. Americans, he knew, would not be willing to fight an Asian war.

Popperfoto

Left: Officials sign the treaty between Japan and Manchukuo (formerly Manchuria) in 1932. The occasion marked the debut of Japan's imperialist policy in China. The United States withheld recognition of the new state. Right: Japan made further inroads into China in 1933. In this photograph, soldiers wave the national flag and shout delightedly after the capture of Shanhaikuan.

The Sino-Japanese War

Meanwhile, the Japanese military continued its preparation to assault China. In December of 1934, steps were taken to free the navy from the limitations imposed at Washington in 1922 and London in 1930. Notice was given that the treaties would not be renewed when they expired in December of 1936. In June of 1935, the Chinese government was forced to withdraw anti-Japanese forces from Hopei, and in November there was formed an East Hopei autonomous regime under Japanese control which stretched from T'ung-chou to the coast. In February of 1936, Japan's premier, Viscount Makoto Saito, was assassinated along with several other ministers by young radical army officers. It was an effort to undo the gains made by liberals in a parliamentary election earlier in the month. Koki Hirota, the new premier, although considered a political moderate, had endeared himself to the military when, as foreign minister in October of 1935, he had proclaimed three points as the basis for his foreign policy—establishment of a Japan-Manchukuo-China bloc, suppression of anti-Japanese activities, and organization of a joint Japanese-Chinese front against the Communists.

The fall of 1936 found the Japanese acting more boldly. In September they levied upon the Chinese government seven secret demands, the most important of which were autonomy for five northern provinces and the appointment of Japanese advisers throughout the Chinese government. Despite a threat of immediate invasion as the penalty for noncompliance, Chiang turned Tokyo away. That show of independence by Nanking disturbed the Japanese. They were even more troubled by a popular campaign among Chinese students and workers in the summer and fall of 1936 to force Chiang to wage an all out war against the Japanese and drive them from the country. Chiang had been concentrating on fighting the Communists while placating the Japanese, and that course was extremely unpopular. Indeed, in December, Chang Hsueh-liang, the war lord in Manchuria, captured the generalissimo and would not release him until he pledged to declare war on Japan. The result was an understanding between the Communists and the Nationalists, in January of 1937, to join hands in battling the invader.

Clearly, Tokyo had to strike before a really united opposition could be formed, and strike they did in July of 1937. On the night of the seventh, Japanese soldiers on maneuvers clashed with Chinese troops by the Marco Polo bridge, about ten miles from Peking. Who fired the first shot and who was responsible for the encounter has

Chiang Kai-shek speaks at a rally in 1937. Although determined to repel the Japanese invaders, Chiang was beset by difficulties. By December 1937 he was in rapid retreat.

Camera Press

never been determined. What is known is that the hostilities signalled the opening of a great war between the two powers which was to last for eight years.

For two and a half weeks following the incident at the bridge there was a truce between the two sides as they attempted to negotiate a settlement. During that time it appeared that the engagement may have been only a minor and isolated one. On July 25, however, fighting broke out at Lanfang, a place midway between Peking and Tientsin, and it became evident that the Japanese army was on the march. On July 28, Peking fell to the Japanese soldiers. Tientsin was taken next day. A large-scale campaign was now undertaken in north China. Throughout the summer and fall the emperor's army occupied key cities—Paoting south of the Peking-Tientsin line in September, Kueisui to the northwest in October, and T'ai-yuan to the southwest in November. Meanwhile, an assault had been begun against Shanghai in August, leading to the fall of that key port on November 8. One month later Nanking, Chiang's capital, was occupied. In rapid succession other key places were conquered—Hangchow in December, Tsingtao in January of 1938, Amoy in May, Canton and Hankow in October. Retreating before the enemy, Chiang finally settled his government in Chungking, deep in the interior.

Thus, by the end of 1938, Japan was in control of most of China's chief coastal cities and railways. Following the precedent six years earlier in Manchuria, Tokyo had, on March 28, 1938, established at Nanking a puppet government called the Reformed Government of the Republic of China. It ruled the area south of the Yellow River. In September, there was created a United Council for China at Peking to administer northern China. It was but a short, and logical, step to the next Japanese move—the announcement of a ''new order'' in eastern Asia based on a ''tripartite relationship of mutual aid and co-ordination between Japan, Manchukuo, and China in political, economic, cultural, and other fields.'' Proclaimed on November 3, 1938, it established the Greater East Asia Co-Prosperity Sphere—the vehicle for the exercise of Japanese hegemony in that vast area.

There followed, slowly but surely, the closing of the Open Door. Western firms had their operations curtailed and, in many cases, they were forced out of business by severe restrictions and discrimination. The day of Caucasian supremacy was over. China was for Asians under Japanese direction.

The port of Shanghai fell to Japan after weeks of fighting in November 1937. These troops are shown firing on Chinese positions in the final stage of the battle.

The Panay Incident

After Shanghai fell to Japan in November 1937, the Chinese capital of Nanking, 130 miles inland to the west, soon came under attack. There on the Yangtze River the United States gunboat *Panay* lay at anchor on December 11. The vessel was one of several patrol craft flying the Stars and Stripes or Union Jack which had authority under an eighty-year-old treaty to patrol the river and protect American and British citizens and their interests in the area.

Lieutenant Commander James Hughes, skipper of the *Panay*, had been instructed to observe American neutrality in the conflict between China and Japan. Most American diplomats had been evacuated earlier, but with Nanking's fall now imminent, the last diplomats and some newsmen boarded the *Panay*. Three American oil tankers were anchored nearby. Hughes decided that the convoy should move upriver out of danger of Japanese shells and bombs. Japanese officials were notified of the vessels' new position, twelve miles north of Nanking.

The following day, a Sunday, dawned fine and clear. Soon after 8 AM, encroaching Japanese fire again prompted Hughes to move on. By noon the four vessels lay anchored a further eighteen miles up river. Again, Japanese authorities were informed of the change in location.

At 1:35 PM the faint drone of aircraft engines caused a stir on board the *Panay*. Planes were spotted high overhead. Then, seconds later, bombs rained about the vessel. Some scored direct hits. The tankers were also damaged.

Once they had recovered their wits, crew members manned the *Panay*'s ten 30-caliber machine guns in a futile attempt to defend the vessel against the Japanese onslaught. More than twenty planes—bombers and fighters—were in the sky. The newsmen began to photograph the attack.

Half an hour later the order to abandon ship was given. The captain's launch and a motorized sampan ferried crew and passengers to the riverbank. With the *Panay* settling in the water, two Japanese patrol boats approached and fired on the stricken vessel. Soldiers boarded it briefly. The *Panay* sank soon after 4 PM. Two crew members had been killed and thirty wounded; an Italian newsman on board also died. Throughout the affair the Stars and Stripes fluttered horizontally and vertically from masts.

Japan claimed the incident was an error, a case of mistaken identity. The Japanese naval commander in China knew nothing about it until after the event. It seems, however, that orders to attack the *Panay* (British patrol boats on the Yangtze were also hit) emanated from the commander of an army regiment in the district, a man with a rabid hatred of Western nations.

Navy Department, National Archives

President Roosevelt voiced America's shock at the premeditated attack on a neutral vessel. A stiff protest was made to the Japanese government. In response to Roosevelt's request, Japan apologized, admitted responsibility, and later agreed to pay $2.2 million in compensation.

The *Panay* incident angered Americans who saw it as an outrageous act by an aggressive nation. But there was no desire for war. The matter, it was felt, could properly be handled by diplomatic means—as it was.

Japan's attack on the American gunboat Panay *made headlines around the world. Three people on board were killed—two crew members and a journalist. Right, from top: Two machine-gunners take aim in a desperate attempt to fight off the aircraft; crew members abandon ship; the last survivors reach the safety of the river bank. Below: The* Panay *settles in the Yangtze.*

The capture in 1937–38 of Nanking (below) and Canton (left) demonstrated the efficiency of Japan's war machine. Although Americans viewed events in the Far East with concern, most did not consider them a direct threat to the security of the United States.

Right and opposite: © Beltrame, Corriere della Sera, Archives Idées & Editions

There was not very much the United States could do about the Japanese takeover of China. Public outrage was very great. Reports in newspapers and newsreels on movie screens telling of repeated attacks on defenseless cities by Japanese aircraft and wanton killings of innocent civilians by Japanese soldiers shocked Americans. The administration shared the sentiments of the American people and both Roosevelt and Hull made no secret of their displeasure. They had not relented on their policy of nonrecognition of Manchukuo and appeared determined to maintain Chinese territorial integrity and equality of commercial opportunity for all nations. Four months before the Marco Polo bridge affair in 1937, Hull had let Japan know that the United States would not turn its back on the Far East. American moral, commercial, and cultural interests in China, he said, were too great to permit any one power to gain control over that country.

Three months after the incident, on October 5, the president himself, in a speech in Chicago, condemned "the present reign of terror and lawlessness." He suggested, too, that the aggressor state ought to be quarantined so as to protect the health of the community. He did not mention Japan by name but there was no doubt to which nation he referred. And the day after the talk, he stated his concurrence in a resolution by the League of Nations

assembly branding Japan as the violator of the Kellogg-Briand Pact and the Nine-Power Treaty.

Beyond a display of indignation, the president did not go. Force, or even measures short of force such as economic sanctions, was not possible. The American people were no more willing in 1938 to fight a war in Asia—or to risk one, for that matter—than they had been in 1932. They had overwhelmingly approved legislation in 1935 and 1937 designed to insulate their country against getting caught in a war such as had happened in 1917. It was not surprising, therefore, that at a meeting of nineteen nations in Brussels, convened in November of 1937 by the Belgian government at the suggestion of the League of Nations to deal with the Asian crisis, the United States (and all the other nations) refused to take drastic action.

All the president did to manifest his abhorrence of the Japanese action in China, and that of the public, was to give help to China without incurring diplomatic complications. In July of 1938, he placed a "moral" embargo on airplanes to Japan by urging American manufacturers to withhold their sale. And at the end of that year, he extended a loan of $25 million to China through the Export-Import Bank. Meanwhile, because Japan did not choose to declare war on China formally, and continued to label the hostilities the "China incident," the neutrality laws were inoperative and American citizens were able to supply China with arms, ammunition, aircraft, and other items useful for fighting.

At the same time, the president continued to let Japan know that the United States would never accept the new order in eastern Asia. In response to the Foreign Office statement establishing the Greater East Asia Co-Prosperity Sphere, and to a subsequent declaration in which Tokyo stated that Japan's aim "in conducting the present vast military campaign" was only to secure "the minimum guarantee needed for the execution by China of her function as a participant in the establishment of the new order," Roosevelt was clear and blunt. On December 30, 1938, he instructed Ambassador Joseph C. Grew to inform the Foreign Office that the United States did not admit "that there is need or warrant for any one power to take upon itself to prescribe what shall be the terms and conditions of a 'new order' in areas not under its sovereignty and to constitute itself the repository of authority and the agent of destiny in regard thereto."

The words were strong, direct, and clear. Unhappily, the president was to learn that words alone would have no effect on Japan. Only by the sword would the island empire be halted in its wayward course. He had begun preparations for that contingency when in January of 1938 he requested of Congress a $1 billion appropriation for a two-ocean navy. Little did he know, however, when he signed the bill in May, that he would be using those vessels three years and seven months later in a life-and-death struggle with Japan.

Chapter 4

THE FASCIST THREAT

The rise of Fascist dictatorships in Europe reinforced the mood of isolationism in the United States. It also gave impetus to the desire to take whatever steps were required to insulate the nation from another possible war. So when the Ethiopian crisis erupted, Congress acted swiftly to ensure neutrality. But when the Spanish Civil War began, so-called neutrality was criticized for preventing assistance to a government under attack from Fascist-supported rebels. President Roosevelt spelled out the significance of Hitler's policies and made decisions which meant that, if the time came to jump down off the fence, the United States would be able to take speedy and effective action.

Storm Clouds over Europe

Though the emergence of an aggressive, expansionist Japan greatly troubled American policy-makers during the 1930s, they regarded concurrent developments in Europe as even more dangerous. The rise of dictatorships —particularly of Hitler Germany—appeared to pose a greater threat to the world power balance and to American security than the actions of the Land of the Rising Sun. It also raised the possibility that the troubles of Europe would lead to a war in which the United States might well become involved unless proper precautions were taken.

For the newly elected Franklin D. Roosevelt, of course, even the storm clouds gathering over Europe were secondary in importance to the desperate economic problems at home. Nonetheless, he could not be wholly indifferent to their appearance and was not inclined to be so, either by temperament or by experience. His predecessor, Herbert Hoover, had left him with two commitments: the United States had delegates at the Geneva Disarmament Conference then in progress, and it

would participate in a world economic conference to be held in London in June 1933.

The Geneva conference had assembled under League of Nations auspices in February 1932, at least in part because of German demands for relief from the military provisions of the Versailles Treaty which put her at the mercy of her stronger neighbors. In order to avoid a major arms race in Europe, most of the nations represented hoped to deal with this issue, not by allowing Germany to expand her armed forces, but by persuading other countries to reduce theirs. By the spring of 1933, however, the conference was deadlocked. France adamantly refused to reduce her armies without guarantees from both Great Britain and the United States that they would come to her assistance in the event of a future German attack. The United States regarded such a guarantee as contrary to her traditional policy against "entangling" alliances. And Great Britain refused to meet

The threat to civilization posed by fascism found expression in grim sketches by George Grosz.
The Ambassador of Good Will, *dated 1936, depicts a fat Nazi and emaciated soldiers in a grisly landscape.*

The Metropolitan Museum of Art, Gift of Priscilla A. B. Henderson

The bespectacled Maksim Litvinov (left, shown arriving for talks at the White House) became Russia's commissar for foreign affairs in 1930 and handled the negotiations which led to the establishment of diplomatic links between the USSR and the USA three years later. At this time, the Soviet dictator, Joseph Stalin (opposite), was viewed with a measure of favor by the West—until the infamous purge trials began after 1936.

AP

the French request without some assurance of American support.

In March, British Prime Minister Ramsay MacDonald tried to break this deadlock with a new plan. He called, among other things, for consultation by the European powers in cases of aggression and for the imposition of military and economic sanctions against any guilty nation. The United States, it was hoped, would cooperate in such a scheme by refusing to sell arms and war supplies to the designated aggressor.

Roosevelt was sympathetic to this proposal. He had already endorsed discretionary arms embargo legislation, then before Congress, which would have made American cooperation possible. In late April, MacDonald and French Premier Édouard Herriot visited Washington to sound out the new president. After some discussion Roosevelt agreed in principle that America would "undertake to refrain from any action . . . which would tend to defeat the collective effort which the States in consultation might have decided upon against the aggressor." His decision was duly announced at Geneva.

This modest departure from traditional nonentanglement policies produced a strong reaction in Congress. The Senate Foreign Relations Committee promptly amended the embargo proposal to make it apply automatically and impartially to all countries at war. Since this would have permitted no distinction to be made between aggressors

and their victims, it was, as Secretary of State Cordell Hull correctly pointed out, "directly in conflict with our proposal at Geneva." Because the Senate could not be easily swayed from its position and Roosevelt was unwilling to risk a confrontation which might have endangered his relief and recovery programs, the whole matter of an embargo was soon dropped. The deadlock at Geneva continued. Germany's delegates withdrew in October 1933 and, for good measure, withdrew from the League of Nations as well. By the summer of 1934 the conference had disbanded. Attempts at European disarmament had come to a full stop.

It is doubtful, given the attitudes of both France and Germany, that firmer action by the United States would have saved the cause of disarmament. But America's stance clearly did nothing to strengthen the position of the European democracies vis-à-vis the totalitarian states. The pattern here fashioned was to be followed for some time to come. Roosevelt was favorably inclined toward collective security arrangements, but he had more urgent priorities. Congress was wary of entanglements, and the president chose to avoid a showdown with the lawmakers for reasons of domestic policy. The result was an essentially weak American position which did little to resolve the problems of Europe or of the world.

The pattern was immediately duplicated at the London Economic Conference. This meeting had been called to discuss such matters as world unemployment, the decline of commodity prices, monetary confusion, lagging international trade, and reparations and war debts. It was hoped, of course, that the nations would be able to agree on constructive joint measures for the solution of at least some of these interrelated problems. Even while agreeing to participate in the conference, Hoover had vetoed any discussion of the debt question. Roosevelt, responding to congressional sentiment against the reduction or cancellation of the Allied obligations stemming from the First World War, concurred. Secretary of State Hull, who headed the American delegation, hoped that at least some reciprocal tariff reduction might be undertaken in order to revive international trade.

Though Roosevelt had promised to introduce legislation necessary for this purpose, he withdrew the promise when he realized that its fulfillment would endanger other New Deal measures. So Hull came to London, as he put it, "with empty hands." That left the conference mainly with the issue of currency stabilization. Here, too, Roosevelt undercut the delegates—including his own—by sending his "bombshell message" of July 3, which labeled their proposal for an eventual return to the gold standard "a catastrophe amounting to world tragedy." Instead, he opted for unilateral devaluation of the dollar, and for currency management to meet national rather than international objectives. The conference disbanded without reaching any major agreement.

As in the case of the Geneva conference, there is no assurance that a different American course would have brought better results. The European powers were no more ready for meaningful international action than was the United States, and John Maynard Keynes, the most famous economist of his day, called Roosevelt's course "magnificently right." But once again the United States had contributed nothing to the solution of world problems. Parochial concerns had frustrated collective action.

The economic conference in London was not entirely without result for the United States, however. It was there that the head of the Russian delegation, Maksim Litvinov, began the talks with American officials that soon led to the establishment of diplomatic relations between the two nations. After the Bolshevik Revolution of 1917, all major countries had withheld formal recognition of the new regime. Germany had broken that solid front in 1922, and within two years virtually all of the others had also exchanged ambassadors with the Soviet Union. The lone important exception remained the United States.

By the onset of the depression, Stalin had firmly established himself as Lenin's successor. Through the policy of "socialism in one country," which found expression in the first Five-Year Plan for economic development, he had apparently exorcised the specter of a Communist world revolution. American sentiment for recognition of the Soviet Union now began to grow.

Business leaders, who had already invested substantial sums in Russia in the 1920s, wanted to safeguard their investments and increase their trade. Holders of Czarist bonds hoped to be able to recoup some of their losses. The influential chairman of the Foreign Relations Committee, Senator William E. Borah, even thought that recognition would further the cause of disarmament.

Roosevelt, on entering the presidency, was sympathetic to these views. He therefore responded to Litvinov's London overtures with a letter to the Soviet president,

Mikhail Kalinin, suggesting "frank and friendly conversations." In November 1933, Litvinov, now commissar for foreign affairs, arrived in Washington, and within nine days he and Roosevelt had reached apparent agreement on all outstanding issues. Though the president may have entertained the hope that American recognition of the Soviet Union would promote global stability by serving as a check on Germany and Japan, he almost certainly acted primarily from domestic motives. An immediate loan by the Reconstruction Finance Corporation to facilitate the Russian purchase of cotton in the United States clearly signaled the basic purpose of the new policy. Subsequent vain attempts to get the Soviets to carry out the Roosevelt-Litvinov agreements concentrated on Russia's failure to repay American bondholders and continued Communist subversion in the United States —two issues having little to do with broad international problems. In any event, US-Soviet relations did not improve materially after recognition was extended, nor did trade between the two nations increase significantly.

The foreign policy actions of the United States thus were weak, narrowly nationalistic, and generally unconstructive in the early days of the Roosevelt administration. Not only did they fail to come to grips with the major problems of the world, they stood in sharp contrast to the vigorous, wide-ranging experimentation shown by the administration in domestic matters. The contrast was not coincidental, for the depression which stimulated and made possible the bold domestic departures of the New Deal promoted, at the same time, the resurgence of a timid and essentially short-sighted American isolationism.

The coming of the depression fostered isolationism in several major ways. It deflated America's confidence in its strength and in its ability to affect world events in a positive and constructive manner. It also increased popular distrust of bankers and of big business, the two groups with the largest direct stake in foreign trade and in maintaining active relations with other nations. The admonition that the United States should confine itself to tilling its own garden became more and more persuasive under these circumstances.

The rise of the European dictators, far from counteracting the development of such sentiments, contributed to their spread. To the fear that "foreign adventures" would undermine America's chances for economic recovery, there was now added the even greater fear that the world was headed for a new war. Unless appropriate and effective steps were taken to insulate the country from the conflict, the United States would sooner or later be involved. Such new worries had already been expressed after the Japanese invasion of Manchuria in September 1931, and particularly after the naming, a month later, of an American representative to join the council of the League of Nations in its consideration of the crisis. They were heightened when the appointment of Adolf Hitler as chancellor of Germany on January 30, 1933, was followed by a program for German rearmament, and when the Fascist leader, Benito Mussolini, began to speak ever more longingly of turning the Mediterranean Sea into an Italian lake.

The advent of the dictators had not, in itself, aroused much concern in the United States. Mussolini's seizure of power on October 30, 1922, had been widely applauded as bringing order out of chaos. His often-expressed imperial ambitions seemed to be satisfied by the temporary capture of the Greek island of Corfu in 1923, and his foreign policy proved to be moderate and generally peaceful thereafter. Accordingly, his image in America became essentially that of a charismatic leader who had saved capitalism and the Catholic church in Italy, drained the Pontine marshes, and made the trains run on schedule. For many American businessmen, *Il Duce* was not only the proper antidote for bolshevism, but the ideal executive who "cut through" and got things done. For some intellectuals, his dynamic pragmatism stood in sharp and welcome contrast to the decadence of middleclass liberalism. Not until Mussolini began to plot the conquest of Ethiopia in 1934 was the faith of most Americans in his essential benevolence shaken. Even then, however, there were those who regarded him as a necessary check on the new ambitions of Nazi Germany.

The appointment of Hitler to the chancellorship also did not unduly alarm the United States at first, although the honeymoon period was much shorter. The democratic Weimar Republic had tried, after the First World War, to pick up the pieces of the defeated German empire. It had struggled manfully, and at times successfully, against the disabilities imposed by the Versailles Treaty, against runaway inflation, and against a multitude of other problems. In these efforts it had had the understanding and support of the United States, but only rarely the enthusiastic backing of its own citizens. It had never persuaded the majority of Germans, nor even the key elements within its own bureaucracy, that it could restore more than a pale shadow of past prosperity and glory.

The onset of the depression cut off the supply of foreign capital, largely from the United States, and thus destroyed the precarious economic balance which Germany had achieved. When a succession of weak governments failed to cope with the ensuing crisis, the German people turned increasingly to Adolf Hitler. By July 1932 his National Socialist German Workers' party had become the largest in parliament. Within six months, the aged President Paul von Hindenburg had been persuaded to ask Hitler to head a new government, and the transformation of the Weimar Republic into the Third Reich got rapidly underway.

Immediate American reaction to these events was generally muted. Germany, after all, was far away, while the depression was right at home. To some Americans, moreover, Hitler was a man of action and a dedicated anti-Communist. His extremism would surely be tempered by the responsibilities of power, and he might prove to be the savior of Europe. But these attitudes were

Exploiting fears aroused by social unrest, Benito Mussolini came to power in 1922 after an unimpeded march on Rome by his Fascist horde; the king then invited him to form a government. His regime soon became an aggressive dictatorship. Opposite top left: Il Duce harangues the crowd. Top right: Recruitment poster for the army transport corps. Bottom: The stocky little dictator salutes passing volunteer soldiers in central Rome.

THE FASCIST THREAT

*Adolf Hitler's National Socialist German Workers'
party rose to prominence in world politics in less
than twenty years. Having whipped up and manipulated
feelings of national pride, racism, and a sense of
destiny at great theatrical rallies, the fuehrer
was appointed chancellor in 1933. Within months, Germany
had virtually become a military dictatorship. Clockwise
from bottom left: Hitler, with President Paul von
Hindenburg, soon after becoming chancellor;
reviewing storm troopers at Nuremburg in 1927;
at Dortmund in 1933; a rally at Nuremberg.*

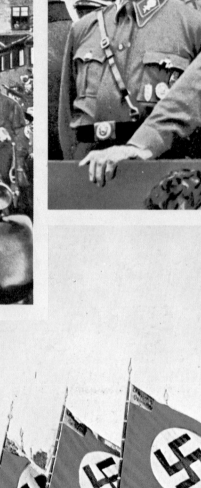

soon replaced by genuine concern. Hitler's continuing use of unbridled rhetoric, his persecution of liberals and Jews, and, above all, his vigorous espousal of a managed economy and of rearmament produced alarm in influential quarters, including official Washington. Within a year, diplomatic dispatches from Berlin would suggest that the fuehrer's solution for Germany's problems included war.

The net effect of the rise of militant dictatorships in Europe was not, however, to stir the United States to effective international action. On the contrary, it produced a further retreat into political isolationism. The feeling that the efforts of Germany and Italy to upset the Versailles settlement might lead to war gave new relevance to some of the ostensible lessons of the First World War. In 1917, it was now widely argued, the United States had intervened in a European war in the mistaken belief that it could make the world safe for democracy and help shape a new international order. Its intervention in fact had produced nothing of the kind. The European powers had acted after the war from the same selfish motives which had produced the war in the first place, motives in no way related to the interests of the United States. These motives had been skillfully obscured by Allied propaganda. America, contrary to its traditional policies and true interests, had been tricked into entering the war. The only Americans whose interests had been served had been bankers and businessmen, who had sought to safeguard their investments and increase their profits by trade in arms and war materials.

The situation developing in Europe by 1934 seemed to most Americans a deadly parallel to the years from 1914 to 1917. The quarrels between the dictators and the European democracies were over the Treaty of Versailles, which incorporated the selfish aims to which America had been opposed. To meddle in these quarrels would serve no useful purpose for the United States. Such action would be likely to create new entanglements and new incidents which might once again give selfish vested interests in America—the same interests whose domestic failure had brought on the depression—the chance to propel the United States into war. A new conflict would be worse than the last one. Not only had advances in technology made war itself more terrible; the United States, weakened by the depression, would find its democratic institutions undermined and would emerge from a new conflict as a dictatorship. American conservatives, already warning that the New Deal was the road to socialism, feared a Communist dictatorship. Liberal and radical Americans, concerned over civil liberties in wartime and over the need for regimentation which they believed modern war to require, foresaw the coming of fascism to America. Both groups saw American involvement in war as a far greater evil than in any other conceivable result of Europe's quarrels. And most Americans, looking on war as total entanglement, sought

*The influential Key
Pittman of Nevada led the
Senate fight for neutrality
laws.*

*Historian Charles A. Beard
gave voice to his isola-
tionist views in* The Devil
Theory of War *(1936).*

*Isolationist Senator Gerald
P. Nye argued that entry
into the First World War had
been disastrous for the USA.*

more than ever to be left alone with their domestic problems.

The rising tide of isolationism was signaled as early as April 1934, when Congress passed the Johnson Debt Default Act, forbidding any American citizen or corporation to lend money to nations in default of their debt payments to the United States. Some of the supporters of this legislation hoped it would pressure the European countries into resuming their payments. But more saw it as a device for preventing the development of financial ties which might eventually involve the United States in European wars. The passage of the Johnson Act followed by only one day the unanimous approval by the Senate of the establishment of a committee to investigate the munitions industry with a view to recommending legislation which would take the profits out of war and thus, presumably, reduce pressures for American involvement. That committee chose the isolationist Senator Gerald P. Nye of North Dakota as its chairman. In nearly two years of activity, it concentrated on trying to demonstrate the folly of America's entry into the First World War and on designing so-called neutrality legislation to prevent a repetition of that catastrophe.

The ground plowed by the Nye committee had already been prepared by a sizable group of journalists and historians, who continued their labors through much of the 1930s. A *Fortune* article, "Arms and the Men," had contributed to the establishment of the committee by castigating international arms dealers as disturbers of

the peace. George Seldes's *Iron, Blood and Profits* and H. C. Engelbrecht and F. C. Hanighen's *Merchants of Death,* both published in 1934, expanded on the theme that the greed and lack of national loyalties of arms manufacturers were potent factors in creating international crises. Even earlier, Harry Elmer Barnes, whose *The Genesis of the World War* appeared in 1926, and his student C. Hartley Grattan, who wrote *Why We Fought* in 1929, had developed the thesis that American entry into the First World War had been brought about, contrary to the country's true interests, by direct and indirect Allied pressure, and by the machinations of bankers, brokers, and businessmen who had unwisely tied American prosperity to the cause of Britain and France.

This "devil theory of war" was widely accepted by a public which overwhelmingly rejected the notion that the United States should again participate in European war. It was implicitly or explicitly supported by a host of other authors. Walter Millis, an editorial writer for the New York *Herald-Tribune,* who had already published a debunking history of the Spanish-American War, produced *Road to War,* which became a Book-of-the-Month Club selection and a best seller in 1935. The book blamed the First World War on "the ceaseless, intricate, and insane game of European diplomacy." It concluded that the United States had been duped into participating by Allied propaganda and its own banking and financial interests. Charles C. Tansill put the same argument in more scholarly terms in a 1938 volume entitled *America Goes to War*. Even Charles A. Beard, perhaps the best-known American historian of the time, gave credence to this view. His *The Devil Theory of War*, which appeared in 1936, was ostensibly designed to show that "war is not the work of a demon . . . [but] our very own work, for which we prepare, wittingly or not, in ways of peace." But Beard was himself an isolationist, and he set forth in great detail the machinations of American businessmen and the pressure they had brought on the Wilson administration. Discounting plausible alternative explanations for America's entry into the First World War, Beard's argument tended to support the very theory he was seeking to discredit.

Such arguments were not only accepted by most American pacifists, but also by groups as diverse as the Socialist party and the American Legion. The National Council for the Prevention of War, the Women's International League for Peace and Freedom, and the National Peace Conference lobbied strenuously for legislation to keep America out of war, and carried on an extensive propaganda campaign as well. Socialist leader Norman Thomas was one of the most ardent and articulate champions of American neutrality. The American Legion and other veterans' groups took the lead in proposing measures "to take the profits out of war." Various student organizations sought to lend emphasis to their peace efforts by subscribing to the Oxford pledge not to serve in any future war. One of the first public opinion polls conducted by George Gallup found 95 per cent of all Americans opposed to involvement in war and in favor of actions designed to avoid it.

Against the flood of isolationist rhetoric and sentiment, the administration saw itself as essentially helpless. Roosevelt himself consistently placed domestic considerations ahead of world problems. He had reneged on his earlier advocacy of the League of Nations during the presidential campaign of 1932. He scarcely mentioned foreign affairs in his first inaugural address and allowed narrowly national concerns to shape his policy at the London Economic Conference. His domestic programs enjoyed the support of most congressional isolationists, and he consistently refused to court what he regarded as political disaster by defying them on matters of foreign policy. Secretary of State Hull was even more anxious to maintain cordial relations with Congress, in which he had served for many years. And the new chairman of the Foreign Relations Committee, Senator Key Pittman of Nevada, was neither a strong leader nor a strong internationalist. Under these circumstances, vigorous American foreign policy initiatives were hardly likely.

Roosevelt made his one serious effort to test domestic waters in January 1935, when the administration reintroduced in the Senate the long-dormant proposal for American adherence to the World Court. That experience only confirmed his belief that any attempt to involve the United States in world affairs would be impolitic.

Although adherence to the World Court would not have committed the United States to any international action, the fear that it would be a prelude to genuine commitments aroused a storm of opposition. Publisher William Randolph Hearst and the popular isolationist radio priest, Father Charles E. Coughlin, promoted a letter-writing

Campaigning publisher William Randolph Hearst supported the move to keep the United States out of the World Court. A fervent isolationist, Hearst brought public pressure to bear on Congress by organizing a write-in campaign. Here he is shown in the elegant surroundings of his home.

campaign which swamped legislators with anticourt sentiment. On the floor of the Senate, Hiram Johnson of California, the author of the Johnson Act, characterized the protocol as another attempt "to meddle and muddle, under an hysterical internationalism, in the controversies that Europe has and that Europe never will be rid of." It will mean, he insisted, "going into the League of Nations as surely as night follows day." These sentiments were echoed over and over again during the debate. In the end, the Senate rejected joining the court by a margin that was almost identical to the tally by which the League of Nations covenant had been defeated in 1920.

Reaction to Events in Ethiopia

American concern over involvement in "European" affairs was brought to a new pitch by the developing conflict between Italy and Ethiopia. Reports that Mussolini planned to conquer the African country "whenever Abyssinia commits an 'overt' act" had reached the State Department as early as September 1934. By December, Italy had manufactured the "overt act," claiming to have been attacked by Ethiopian forces at the Wal Wal waterhole in the Ogaden desert. Shortly thereafter, the American chargé d'affaires in Addis Ababa reported that Emperor Haile Selassie was considering asking for mediation. Hull moved at once to discourage such a request. He informed the emperor that, though the United States followed all efforts to settle the dispute "with sympathetic interest," it "could not usefully or properly take *any* action."

Indeed, the heating up of the situation in the Mediterranean only spurred efforts to ensure American neutrality. The State Department had been engaged in drafting some sort of neutrality legislation since early 1934, but was undecided on the degree of discretion which should be left to the president in the application of embargoes, travel bans, loan prohibitions, and similar matters. On March 19, 1935, Roosevelt, disregarding the advice of Hull and trying, perhaps, to speed up the decision-making process in the State Department, met with the Nye committee. Although he could hardly have been unaware of the isolationist character of the committee, the president urged it to consider the whole question of neutrality with a view to introducing appropriate legislation. The committee responded eagerly to this suggestion. By early summer it had produced proposals for mandatory, inflexible bans on the sale of arms and ammunition to belligerents in international conflicts, as well as for bans on loans and on travel on ships owned by any warring party.

Hull took public issue with these proposals. He urged a discriminatory arms embargo which would have

allowed the United States to cooperate with possible League of Nations sanctions against Italy. At the same time, however, he rejected still another appeal by Haile Selassie that the United States take a more positive role in seeking a peaceful settlement of the dispute. Roosevelt privately supported Hull's position. He approved a resolution calling for presidential discretion in the application of any neutrality law. But this resolution, which the State Department wanted to send to the Foreign Relations Committee, was never publicly aired because Chairman Pittman informed the president's secretary that "if he wants this done, I will introduce it . . . but he will be licked as sure as hell." Worried about the possible fate of the Guffey coal act and other domestic legislation then before Congress, Roosevelt again chose not to fight.

Congress for its part was anxious to act before a war broke out. It passed the Neutrality Act of 1935, including the mandatory arms embargo against all belligerents in international conflicts, on August 23. In approving this legislation, Roosevelt stressed the American commitment both "to the maintenance of peace and the avoidance of any entanglements which would lead us into conflict." He expressed the hope, however, that Congress would give the subject more complete consideration when the embargo provision expired in February 1936.

Though both Roosevelt and Hull clearly doubted that the Neutrality Act was an effective scheme for avoiding war, they were no more prepared than Congress to take positive international action. Five days before the passage of the act, Hull did send, in the president's name, a message to Mussolini. In it he expressed the American hope for a peaceful resolution of the conflict and characterized the possible outbreak of war as a calamity. But when the Italian dictator replied that it was too late to avoid armed conflict, no further American initiatives were undertaken. Haile Selassie's last desperate effort to give the United States a tangible stake by granting an oil concession to a subsidiary of the Standard Vacuum Oil Company resulted only in State Department pressure on officials of the company to terminate the concession at once. On October 3, 1935, Italian forces invaded Ethiopia, and on October 5 the United States declared its neutrality.

For the League of Nations, meeting in Geneva, the Italo-Ethiopian War was a matter of life or death. If the member states, having already failed to take a strong position on the Sino-Japanese conflict, countenanced Italy's naked aggression, the league's intended peace-keeping function would be fatally undermined. Prodded by Great Britain, the league condemned Mussolini's actions on October 5, and barred arms shipments to Italy six days later. The real problem lay elsewhere, however. Mussolini needed no outside arms for the conquest of Ethiopia, but he did need certain strategic materials, particularly oil. Roosevelt had recognized this, and his neutrality message had attempted to discourage all trade

Radio Times Hulton Picture Library

Keystone

Mussolini began preparations for the conquest of Ethiopia in 1932, just nine years after he had sponsored Ethiopian membership in the League of Nations. Emperor Haile Selassie (left, at the league) gained little effective help when he protested Italy's clearly aggressive intentions. The Italian buildup continued throughout 1935 as troops set out from Rome for East Africa (above). The invasion was launched, without declaration of war, on October 3, 1935.

The scarcely trained and poorly armed Ethiopian forces were no match for the well-drilled Italian divisions equipped with armored cars, modern guns, and air support. Addis Ababa fell on May 5, 1936, and four days later Mussolini proclaimed a new Italian empire incorporating Ethiopia. Below: An Ethiopian soldier aims an antitank gun. Bottom left: Italian soldiers establish radio contact before an attack. Right: Invading troops cross the Tacazze River. Bottom right: Ethiopian cavalry lined up for review in 1935.

Radio Times Hulton Picture Library

Keystone

Keystone

Brown Brothers

with belligerents. The president continued to press this "moral embargo" in the face of obvious noncompliance. And Hull, on November 15, called the increasing trade in oil, copper, trucks, scrap iron, and scrap steel "contrary to the policy of this Government" and "to the general spirit of the recent neutrality act." Nonetheless, the value of American exports of petroleum products to Italy and her colonies soon reached more than five times the average for the years 1932–34.

At Geneva, where the League of Nations was debating an embargo on oil shipments, the situation was complex. Both the British and French were reluctant to push the matter of sanctions to the point where Italy might retaliate. They were concerned over Mussolini's indication to the French that he would regard an oil embargo as a military sanction which could have unforseeable consequences. Both countries were also aware that an oil embargo would be ineffective without the cooperation of the United States, and both doubted that such cooperation would be forthcoming. "I cannot," French Foreign Minister Pierre Laval told the Chamber of Deputies on December 28, "prejudge the decision which will be taken by Congress, the authority which will or will not be given to Roosevelt, the usage which Roosevelt will or will not make of his powers." Although he was clearly using America's position as an excuse for his own reluctance to act firmly, Laval's statement was given credibility by the announced policy of the United States. Had Congress proceeded to authorize the president to embargo certain raw materials, that credibility would have been diminished, and those league members actively supporting sanctions might have found some encouragement. Such was not to be the case, however.

In his annual message to Congress on January 3, 1936, Roosevelt called for a "twofold neutrality" program. This would have continued the nondiscriminatory arms embargo but also allowed the president to limit trade in strategic materials with any belligerent to prewar levels. It was a modest proposal. Hoping to win quick congressional approval, Roosevelt sacrificed once again the idea of a discretionary arms embargo and sought no authority to prevent, but only one to limit, other trade with belligerents. Still, it was more than Congress would allow. After heated discussion, and with time running out, a new law was approved which extended the arms embargo in its original form for another year and made American neutrality policy even more rigid. A ban on loans to belligerents was added, as was the requirement that the arms embargo be extended to any nation that might join a war already in progress. Far from making the task of the league easier, therefore, the United States restated its refusal to participate in any trade embargo and, in effect, threatened the league powers with an arms embargo if they decided to intervene in Ethiopia. Roosevelt signed the 1936 Neutrality Act without adverse comment.

It is unlikely, of course, that the League of Nations would have passed the crucial test posed by Mussolini's aggression in any event. There can be little doubt, however, that the clear refusal of the United States to associate itself with the efforts at collective action for peace which were underway at Geneva made the work there more difficult and contributed to its failure. Moreover, it placed America in the anomalous position of supporting, however unintentionally, Mussolini's aggressive designs. Although public opinion favored Ethiopia, the overriding fear of involvement had caused America to cut off the supply of arms with which Ethiopia might have defended itself, while supplying Italy with the oil its war machine needed.

Ominous Developments in Europe

Two weeks after the passage of the second neutrality act, Germany, in clear violation of the Versailles Treaty and of the Locarno Pact of 1925, remilitarized the Rhineland. Though Roosevelt had, in January, publicly castigated those nations "dominated by the twin spirits of autocracy

and aggression," he had also defined the American response as "a well-ordered neutrality" and an "adequate defense to save ourselves from embroilment and attack." Both Roosevelt and the State Department now refused to be drawn into the Rhineland imbroglio, insisting that the United States had neither been party to the Locarno arrangements nor to the violated portion of the Versailles Treaty. The United States maintained this position even when the French premier, Pierre-Étienne Flandin, appealed for at least moral support. Left to their own devices, the European powers tamely acquiesced in what, at least in retrospect, was the clearest step yet taken toward a new world war.

The spring and summer of 1936 were filled with other ominous developments. The London Naval Conference, which had convened the previous December in hopes of checking Japanese naval expansion and dampening the European arms race, broke up in failure on March 25. Five weeks later, Mussolini concluded his conquest of Ethiopia and had King Victor Emmanuel III proclaimed emperor. On July 17, a group of Spanish generals in Morocco set out, under the leadership of Francisco Franco, to overthrow the Republican government and plunged Spain into bitter civil war.

American reaction to these events was in keeping with previous policy. Characteristically, the United States was most seriously involved in the issue of naval disarmament. Roosevelt hoped to the bitter end for at least a "gentlemen's agreement" with Italy, Germany, and Japan that they give notice before beginning a naval buildup. In the final analysis, however, the failure of the London conference only heightened the American sense that the danger of war was growing and that American attempts to intervene in efforts to prevent it were likely to be of little use. The conquest and annexation of Ethiopia were generally deplored. The United States refused to recognize it formally and urged other nations to adopt a similar course. But the United States ended its arms embargo against Italy and Ethiopia on June 16, even before the League of Nations officially conceded its failure by lifting the sanctions it had imposed. It was the Spanish Civil War, however, which revealed the shortcomings of American policy most clearly.

Whereas the Italo-Ethiopian War had been an international conflict in which the danger of involvement for other countries, including the United States, was relatively small, the fighting in Spain was internationalized almost at once. Italy had supplied arms and ammunition

In 1935, Hitler introduced conscription and began a massive drive to rearm Germany in defiance of the Versailles Treaty. Left: A German pilot undergoes training in a glider. Right: The battlecruiser Scharnhorst *is launched in 1936.*

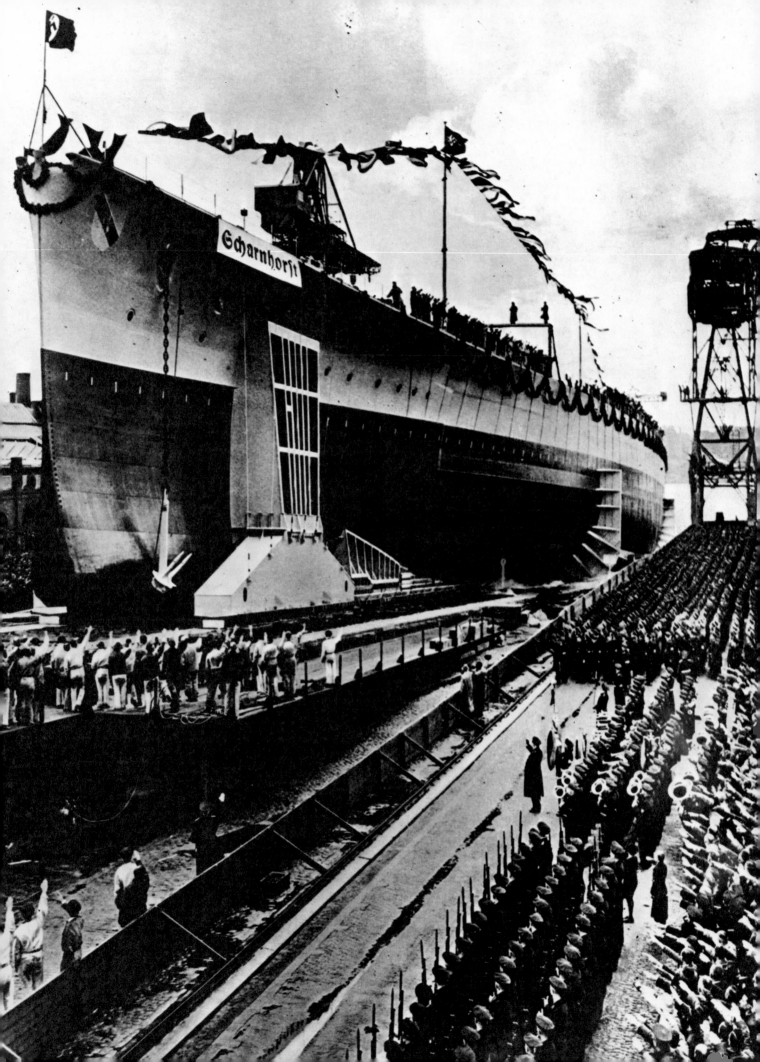

Scharnhorst

Fighting for Spain

On July 17, 1936 the army in Spanish Morocco revolted against the Madrid government of Premier Santiago Quiroga. At once, the ensuing civil war spread to the mainland. It soon became transformed into a conflict between Right and Left, and a major demonstration of Fascist might in Europe. Germany and Italy pledged support to the Nationalist rebels under General Francisco Franco, while the Soviet Union sided with the left-wing Republican government. American opinion also ran strongly in favor of the Republicans. In December 1938, a public opinion poll claimed that 76 per cent of Americans supported the Republicans of Spain—but 79 per cent agreed with Roosevelt's embargo on the sale of arms to both sides.

Stalin proclaimed that liberating Spain from "the yoke of Fascist aggression is not the private concern of Spaniards alone, but the common cause of progressive humanity." Communists in Europe and the United States rallied to the cause. They began recruiting international brigades of foreign volunteers to take up arms for the republic. In all, about 45,000 foreigners served on the Republican side in Spain; Frenchmen, numbering 10,000, made up the largest single group. Although the brigades were Communist-led and comprised a hefty majority of party members and sympathizers, other anti-Fascists and democratic Socialists also answered the call. Some 3,200 Americans served, and aid worth an estimated $2 million found its way, despite the law, to pro-Republican forces. No American is thought to have fought for the Nationalists.

Why did Americans volunteer? Their motives ranged from the almost automatic response of some Communists to the belief of a sizable number of Negroes that fascism meant extreme racism. To the Communist poet Edwin Rolfe, the war echoed American experience:

Spain is yesterday's Russia,
    tomorrow's China,
Yes, and the thirteen seaboard states.

In the United States, the Communist party raised funds and recruited men. Money was collected by "front" organizations and volunteers were recruited surreptitiously by party workers.

The first Americans destined for Spain sailed from New York on December 26, 1936. They formed part of the XV International Brigade along with British, Canadian, and Yugoslav volunteers, but they soon established their own identity as the Abraham Lincoln Battalion. Few had had experience of war; some were teenagers who had never handled a rifle before.

In February 1937 the Americans saw their first action at Jarama. The initial squad had had five weeks of intermittent training; the 400 or so who arrived from the Bronx Young Communist League in

The war in Spain heralded a wider conflict; it has been called the dress rehearsal for the Second World War. Below: American volunteers enlist. Right: A Republican poster calls for support from Spanish youth. Far right: General Francisco Franco, who led the successful revolt, speaks to his troops. Bottom right: Soldiers of an international brigade enjoy hot soup during a lull in the fighting.

Keystone

February were given three days. Two rifle companies were equipped with Remington-style weapons of pre-1914 vintage; another company was issued with machine guns that continually jammed. The Americans took up a reserve position on a ten-mile front where the Nationalists were trying to cut the Madrid-Valencia highway in order to starve Madrid into submission.

Moved to the front line later, the Lincolns found themselves confronted by murderous machine-gun fire. Inexperienced and given only token support by Soviet tanks, they failed to sustain a coordinated attack against enemy trenches. Their ragged advance was soon halted. Initial high spirits were shattered, and the first desertions occurred.

The battalion was next scheduled to undertake a diversion by attacking the enemy along the San Martin Road, while the main thrust concentrated on a nearby hill. Fresh recruits arrived, boosting the battalion's strength to about 450. Air and tank support, although promised, never arrived. The Americans walked into a wall of bullets; their "advance" lasted a mere ten minutes. In battle for less than a week, they now had fewer than a hundred fit men.

A further influx of recruits soon led to the formation of a second battalion, the George Washington. The overflow became part of a third, the Mackenzie-Papineau, which included Canadians.

On July 2, the Americans headed for action once more, this time to take part in a drive aimed at lifting the siege of Madrid. Ordered into the Guadarrama Valley west of the city in 100° heat, they lacked food and adequate ammunition. Nevertheless, on July 7 they entered an enemy-held village which they helped to capture. A week later they abandoned an attempt to take Mosquito Hill. Losses

TODA LA JUVENTUD
UNIDA POR LA PATRIA

had been heavy, so heavy, in fact, that the Washington battalion merged with the Lincoln. After a further failure to wrest the hill from the Nationalists, the Americans withdrew from the front. In less than three weeks their numbers had been reduced from 800 to 300. And Franco's men had not been driven back.

The Aragon front, northeast of Madrid, was the next area of American involvement. In late August, the XV Brigade captured the town of Quinto. For the first time the Lincolns had acted as an effective fighting force. Soon afterwards, they took Belchite with a loss of twenty-three men. In the drive toward Zaragoza in October, they were again victims of incompetent strategy by the brigade leaders, most of whom were east Europeans. In this action—their first—the Mackenzie-Papineau Battalion lost sixty men.

In January 1938 the brigade joined in defending the city of Teruel, seventy miles from the Mediterranean coast. But after a terrible hammering from the air, the Americans withdrew on February 3. In this action their losses numbered some 250.

They were back in Belchite in March, but their attempt to establish defensive positions west of the town was repulsed. Belchite itself came under pressure. The Americans were now in retreat before a major Nationalist drive. Scores of men deserted. One, who had tried to flee on a

Robert Capa/Magnum

previous occasion, was again recaptured —and executed.

By this time, the flow of new American recruits had stopped. Spaniards took their place. From July to September the Americans were thrown into a disintegrating Republican line. Victory was only a dream: the cry now was "To Resist Is to Win." In September the Spanish premier announced that all foreign soldiers would be repatriated. At that stage, the Lincolns numbered about 300, only a quarter of whom were American.

In mid-December, the first American survivors from the Abraham Lincoln Battalion to return home disembarked at New York. About half of the 3,200 volunteers had been killed. On March 28, 1939 Franco's men marched into Madrid, and the republic surrendered the next day. Three days later, on April 1, the United States formally recognized Spain's new Fascist government.

Opposite: In one of the most famous battlefield photographs of all time; Robert Capa caught the moment of death for a Republican soldier. Below: Ernest Hemingway, who was a war correspondent in Spain, is shown with an American volunteer and a photographer. Bottom: These captured men were from the Abraham Lincoln Battalion. They were exchanged in 1938 for captives from the Nationalist side.

Brown Brothers

US Information Agency, National Archives

to the rebels even before their uprising and in the course of time contributed some $400 million and 50,000 men to Franco's forces. Hitler, too, decided to throw Germany's weight on the rebel side and eventually contributed about half as much as Italy. To a lesser degree, the Soviet Union and Mexico came to the aid of the Republican government. Britain and France responded to these developments by setting up the International Non-intervention Committee, which met in London in September and secured pledges from twenty-seven nations not to intervene in the Spanish Civil War. Hypocritically, Italy, Germany, and the Soviet Union participated in the work of the committee.

The United States never signed the nonintervention pledge, and thus maintained its independence of the league powers. Cordell Hull, instead, asked Americans to follow the lead of their government and "scrupulously refrain from any interference whatsoever in the unfortunate Spanish situation." In thus suggesting that a "moral embargo" should be applied to both sides in the conflict, he expressed America's intention to deny arms to the legitimate government of Spain and to place it, in that respect, on the same footing with the rebels seeking its overthrow. In a speech at Chautauqua on August 14, Roosevelt not only praised the "new weapons" which Congress had given him to keep America out of war, but castigated those Americans "who, seeking immediate riches—fool's gold—would attempt to break down or evade our neutrality."

The administration undoubtedly adopted this stance, in part, as a painless and, for once, popular method of cooperation with Britain and France in the maintenance of peace. Roosevelt, moreover, acted in the mistaken belief that to permit arms to be shipped to Spain would aid Franco, whose forces controlled most of the shipping. But it is equally true that the president still regarded avoidance of war as more important than stopping Fascist aggression. He was, therefore, unwilling to take positive action which might lead to involvement. The State Department turned down a Uruguayan proposal that the American republics jointly offer to mediate the war in Spain and informed the Spanish ambassador that the United States would do nothing to aid his government. By the end of 1936, Roosevelt had reached the conclusion that the Neutrality Act of 1936, which still applied only to international conflicts, was defective in that respect and that its arms embargo provisions should be applied to the civil war in Spain. Legislation to that effect passed the Senate by a vote of 81–0 and the House of Representatives by 411–1 after only the briefest discussion. Roosevelt's signing of the measure on January 8, 1937 was applauded in the German press and characterized by General Franco as "a gesture we Nationalists shall never forget."

The American government remained on this course even after it became painfully apparent that Germany and Italy were openly and boastfully violating their nonintervention pledges, and that American neutrality policy was aiding their cause. Roosevelt invoked the embargo provision covering civil wars in the Neutrality Act of 1937 on May 1, the very day the act became effective. He turned down repeated suggestions that the Spanish embargo be rescinded. He also opposed the idea that, in all fairness, it should be extended to Italy and Germany as participants in the conflict. American "neutrality" remained in effect until April 1, 1939, when the United States recognized the Franco regime and agreed to establish diplomatic relations with it.

The policy of noninvolvement with respect to Spain and the adoption of so-called permanent neutrality legislation in the early summer of 1937 marked the high-water line of American isolationism. The Neutrality Act of 1937 expanded the prohibitions of the previous acts. Automatic bans were placed on the arming of American merchant ships trading with belligerents, on travel by American citizens on vessels owned by belligerents, and on the soliciting, by nations or factions at war, of funds or contributions from American citizens. The president could, at his discretion, also close American territorial waters to belligerent submarines and armed merchantmen, and, through a two-year cash-and-carry provision, bar the shipment of specified strategic materials to nations at war, unless title had passed to the purchaser and the transport was accomplished in non-American ships. More than any previous legislation, this measure was testimony to the determination of the United States to insulate itself against "other people's wars."

The Retreat from Isolation

Yet, the summer of 1937 also produced the tentative beginning of what was to become a significant shift in American attitudes and policies. That shift had its origins in two factors. By 1937 the worst effects of the depression had been overcome. Domestic problems seemed to be on their way to solution, and Roosevelt could even contemplate the cutting back of federal spending. Pressure for new legislation to combat the crisis had drastically diminished. Both the government and the public therefore had more time and more energy to devote to matters beyond America's boundaries. At the same time, of course, foreign developments were becoming increasingly threatening. Not only had Japan, Italy, and Germany by that time given evidence of aggressive intent, they had, so far, been successful in their efforts and were showing signs of merging into a powerful bloc aimed at upsetting the existing world balance. On October 25, 1936, Germany and Italy had reached an agreement which laid the basis for future cooperation, and just one month later, Germany and Japan had concluded the Anti-Comintern Pact. The danger that the three powers would merge into a Rome-Berlin-Tokyo axis had become very real. Moreover, the threat of a global conflict, triggered by their individual or collective acts of aggression, was underlined when, after an incident at the Marco Polo bridge near Peking on July 7, 1937, Japan resumed its full-scale war against China.

Roosevelt now became genuinely concerned about the danger of war. For the first time he thought seriously about American action to prevent it. The neutrality debate of the preceding years and the effects of the resulting legislation furthered his thinking along those lines. American policy had helped Mussolini, at least theoretically, and was now helping Franco—in both instances contrary to America's real interest. Were the new law to be applied to the Sino-Japanese conflict, it would undoubtedly help Japan—once again contrary to American interest. In part at least on the basis of such considerations, Roosevelt chose not to invoke the Neutrality Act against China and Japan. This decision, and the muted objections to it, even from many confirmed isolationists, indicated a significant change in sentiment.

The debates over neutrality legislation had themselves produced a split among congressional isolationists. Most legislators had become painfully aware of the fact that American policy, regardless of its nature and intent, was a factor in international controversies. They were no longer as certain as they once had been that neutrality legislation would in fact insulate the nation from war. So dedicated an isolationist as Norman Thomas had argued eloquently against the Spanish embargo because, for all its insulating qualities, it helped the Fascists. In the same vein, some isolationists had opposed the cash-and-carry provision because it would tend to help the major maritime powers, Britain, France, and Japan, in any future wars. The logic of the argument that any blanket policy would have unpredictable, and possibly harmful, results in specific cases thus began to make converts and increased the administration's room for maneuver.

On October 5, 1937, Roosevelt made the first clearcut effort to warn his countrymen against the dangers from abroad and to suggest that positive American action was required to forestall them. In a speech in Chicago he pointed to an epidemic of international lawlessness which threatened established order and justice. "If those things come to pass in other parts of the world," he warned, "let no one imagine that America will escape, that it may expect mercy, that this Western Hemisphere will not be attacked." The president offered no specific program to deal with the situation. But he clearly suggested that the peace-loving nations of the world must cooperate to quarantine the 10 per cent that were threatening international order.

This so-called Quarantine Speech received a mixed, and largely unfavorable, response in the American press. It aroused a strongly negative reaction among congressional isolationists. Nor did it initially impress foreign leaders. The new British prime minister, Neville Chamberlain, pointed out that the United States was supplying 75 per cent of Franco's oil, as well as 65 per cent of Japan's oil and 95 per cent of its scrap metal. He privately offered the opinion that "it is always best to count on nothing from the Americans but words." Roosevelt himself played down the significance of his own remarks by telling a news conference that what he had suggested was not incompatible with neutrality. One man who knew better, however, was the newly appointed German ambassador in Washington, Hans Heinrich Dieckhoff. In his reports to Berlin he conceded that isolationism was still dominant in America "at least for the time being," and that the Quarantine Speech was not likely to lead to an immediate activation of foreign policy. But he also saw in the speech a clear indication that "the jump from isolationism to activism will not be a big one," and that in the event of a war involving Great Britain "the weight of the United States of America would be thrown on the English side of the scale."

Roosevelt hoped to follow up his Chicago statement with a further foreign policy initiative. Following a suggestion by the under-secretary of state, Sumner Welles, he proposed to call for a world conference on international problems at a meeting of the diplomatic corps on Armistice Day, November 11. He intended to ask the various governments to come forward with proposals setting forth the essential principles of international conduct and the means by which armaments might be limited and economic security and stability promoted. In the event of a positive response the United States would assist a ten-nation "executive committee" in working out tentative proposals for submission to all nations as a basis for universal agreement. Roosevelt hoped that this plan would deter, or at least isolate, the totalitarian states, encourage smaller nations to resist aggression, and arouse world public opinion. Most of all, he hoped it would strengthen the position, and the resolve, of Great Britain and France.

His optimism was not shared by Hull, nor by others of his closest advisers, who dissuaded him from making any public announcement without having obtained agreement from the Western democracies. Roosevelt delayed, but on January 12, 1938, he secretly sounded out the views of Great Britain on a similar but somewhat more modest scheme. Chamberlain had by now launched his own plan for reaching agreement with the dictators. It was a plan which included both economic concessions and the recognition of Italy's conquest of Ethiopia in return for assurances on armaments and boundaries. In consequence, the prime minister rejected Roosevelt's proposals on the

The Last Flight of the Hindenburg

"It's broken into flames! It's flashing—flashing! It's flashing terribly! It's bursting into flames and falling on the mooring mast. . . ."

The anguished voice of Herb Morrison and the catastrophe he witnessed are among the most vivid images of the 1930s for those who can remember. Morrison was a commentator for the Chicago radio station WLS, and in the early evening of May 6, 1937 he was describing for his listeners the awesome sight as the airship *Hindenburg* descended slowly toward her mooring mast at

The Hindenburg *tragedy was a terrifying spectacle. Opposite: Ground crew race to safety as the blazing airship plunges into the ground. Below: Most victims were German. The coffins, draped in swastikas, were shipped back to Germany for burial.*

Lakehurst, New Jersey. The huge swastika-emblazoned airship, pride of Nazi Germany, had just completed her first North Atlantic crossing of the new season. At least it seemed as though she had completed it. Mooring ropes were in the hands of ground crew scarcely a hundred feet below. The airship's illustrious older stablemate *Graf Zeppelin*, two days out from Rio de Janeiro bound for Frankfurt, had just received a radio message from the *Hindenburg* announcing safe arrival at Lakehurst. And, as Morrison informed his audience, "Passengers are looking out of the windows waving. . . ." It was a few seconds after 7:25.

In the international atmosphere of the late 1930s it was virtually impossible for anything connected with the German Reich to avoid political and emotional overtones. In the case of the Zeppelin

Airline Company this was unfortunate, since the genius responsible for its existence, Hugo Eckener, was no friend of nazism. And Eckener was much admired, even hero-worshipped, in the United States, where he had received the traditional tickertape parade down Wall Street after flying the *Graf Zeppelin* across the Atlantic in 1928. But in 1937 his great prestige was not sufficient to protect his airships from the taint of nazism. There were certainly people in America who hated the sight of the *Hindenburg* enough to destroy her. And, probably more to the point, Eckener was unable to get American helium, and the *Hindenburg* was therefore inflated with the highly flammable hydrogen.

So it was that the 800-foot-long airship arrived at Lakehurst, with ninety-seven on board including crew. For two-and-a-half days the passengers had been cosseted in luxury not far short of that provided on a Cunard liner: electric heating and hot and cold running water in each of the twenty-five two-berth cabins; a spacious dining room and saloon—equipped with an aluminum baby grand piano; breathtaking views from the promenade deck; even a bar and smoking room ingeniously sealed off against a possible escape of hydrogen.

At 7:25 hydrogen was escaping, nowhere near the smoking room but near the stern. Morrison and all but a handful did not see the small licking flame, but they saw its sequel moments later. First a tremendous sheet of flames from the stern, then the deafening thunder of continuous explosion as 7 million cubic feet of hydrogen lit up the sky. The mighty *Hindenburg* fell, stern first, girders from the frame snapping like matchsticks and slicing murderously through the air, people racing from under the inferno—spectators, ground crew, somehow even passengers and crew. It took only half a minute and claimed thirty-six lives, although the miracle was that so many escaped.

The cause of the tragedy is to some extent still shrouded in mystery. The official board of inquiry—which included Eckener—concluded that it was a freak accident: hydrogen had somehow escaped and been ignited by static electricity. It was impossible, of course, to prove this, and there were—and are—many in Germany and America who preferred a sabotage explanation. In any case, the *Hindenburg* was dead, and with it the age of passenger airships.

grounds that they would delay consideration of specific problems which had to be resolved "if appeasement were to be achieved." The British government withdrew its objections later at the insistence of the foreign secretary, Anthony Eden, who had always hoped to secure American cooperation. By that time, however, the opportunity for such an initiative had passed and the battle lines in Europe hardened. By that time, too, the Nine-Power Conference in Brussels, which, with American participation, had made a final attempt to halt armed Japanese expansion in East Asia, had failed.

In February 1938, Hitler had made himself commander in chief of the German army. He had also replaced the conservative foreign minister, Konstantin von Neurath, with one of his own henchmen, Joachim von Ribbentrop. He had further decided, though the world did not yet know it, to proceed with the annexation of Austria. In the face of such developments, the Welles peace plan was no longer a realistic proposal, if indeed it had ever been one. More than that, though American rhetoric had become more activist, there had been no indication that talk would be backed by deeds. During the Brussels conference, the State Department had repeatedly rejected the suggestion of the American delegate that efforts be launched to modify or repeal the neutrality legislation so as to give credibility to America's new stance.

The neutrality debate of the 1930s had revived interest in a proposal, first made in 1917, that any American declaration of war should be based on a popular referendum. An obscure congressman from Indiana, Louis Ludlow, had championed this legislation since his arrival in Congress and had a bill to that effect in committee in late 1937. When the fear of American involvement in war was temporarily heightened by the sinking of the gunboat *Panay* by Japanese aircraft in Chinese waters on December 12, enough congressmen signed a petition to require the House of Representatives to consider taking up the matter. Roosevelt was sufficiently concerned by this turn of events to send a letter to William B. Bankhead, Speaker of the House, attacking the referendum proposal, and Bankhead left the chair to voice his own objections. In the end, Ludlow's motion to bring the question to the floor was defeated, but only by twenty-one votes. Though it is likely that the proposal itself would have been turned down by a more substantial margin, the vote was an uncomfortable reminder to the administration that its room for maneuver was not yet very great.

Public opinion in the United States, on which Congress and the president ultimately depended for support, had begun to change, however, primarily under the impact of the words and deeds of the leaders of Nazi Germany. As early as March 1937, New York's mayor, Fiorello H. La Guardia, had publicly called Hitler "that brown-shirted fanatic who is now menacing the peace of the world." And two months later the influential archbishop of

VOLK WILL ZU VOLK UND BLUT ZU BLUT DEM FÜHRER DEIN Ja

Bundesarchiv, Koblenz

Hitler's annexation of Austria in 1938 shocked the world. Above: A Nazi handbill hails the union with the words: "People to people and blood to blood. Support your fuehrer." Opposite: German troops march through the streets of Vienna.

Chicago, Cardinal Mundelein, referred to him as "an Austrian paperhanger, and a poor one at that." Mundelein's further denunciation of "loud-mouthed German propagandists" and Germany's "crooked Minister of Propaganda" drew approving comments from the Episcopal bishop of Chicago, the president of the American Federation of Labor, and from George Meany, head of the New York State Federation of Labor. When Ambassador William E. Dodd returned from Berlin in August, he announced that "a basic objective of some powers is to frighten, even destroy democracy everywhere." By the end of the year, the change in public sentiment had begun to worry the German ambassador in Washington. "We should remember," he warned his superiors, "that the development of American public opinion against us was disastrous for us once before, and that only 20 years ago."

Growing American concern that developments in

Germany in particular posed a threat to peace and democracy everywhere took even more concrete form when Hitler's annexation of Austria on March 12, 1938 began a year of almost constant crisis. That action had wiped an independent country from the map of Europe. It could not easily be excused as an effort to remedy the injustice of the Versailles Treaty. The naked use of force raised fears that this method might soon be used again by the German dictator.

The annexation of Austria was, of course, a direct rebuff to the policies of Chamberlain, who only a month before had determined on serious negotiations with Hitler as a way to preserve peace. The commitment to "appeasement" had brought the resignation of the British foreign secretary, Anthony Eden, and thus reduced the prospects of Anglo-American cooperation. It obviously had no restraining effect whatever on the dictators. The German Foreign Office now rejected British and French protests as "inadmissible," and Mussolini refused even to receive mild feelers with regard to possible joint action.

In the United States, the dominant reaction to Hitler's move was one of outrage. "I do not know," Dieckhoff reported to Berlin, "whether in other parts of the world the reunification with Austria has produced such a fantastic hate campaign by the press as the one which has made itself felt here for the last eight days." He lamented the end of America's "true neutrality." The State Department shared the sense of outrage to a considerable degree, but was not yet prepared for meaningful changes in American policy. Roosevelt made that clear

to his major advisers, and Hull told the National Press Club that however much he deplored rampaging international lawlessness, the United States had no intention of "policing the world." Still, the spring of 1938 brought some indications of new American concern.

The United States insisted, for example, that Germany honor Austrian debt agreements, and when this was refused, ostentatiously struck Austria from the list of most-favored nations. Roosevelt allowed the secretary of the interior, Harold Ickes, to win his quixotic but symbolic battle to refuse the sale of helium to Germany on the grounds that it might be used for military purposes. Most important of all, Congress passed the Vinson Naval Expansion Act in May 1938. Under that measure, the expenditure of $1 billion was authorized over the next decade in order to create a navy presumably strong enough to meet the combined fleets of Japan, Germany, and Italy. The margins of passage were 2 to 1 in the Senate and nearly 3 to 1 in the House of Representatives.

In the meantime, it had become clear that Czechoslovakia was to be Hitler's next target. Prompted by Berlin, the German minority clustered in the Sudeten districts had made demands for autonomy on the Prague government which, if granted, would have destroyed both Czechoslovakia's political sovereignty and its military defenses. Germany insisted that the districts in question be "reunited" with the Reich, and moved twelve divisions to the border. The French, bound by an alliance to come to the aid of the Czechs in case of war, now urged the British to support them in checking German ambitions.

Neville Chamberlain returns to Britain from the Munich meeting on September 30, 1938. Waving the piece of paper bearing Hitler's signature, Chamberlain declared he had brought "peace in our time."

Chamberlain, however, was still convinced that "appeasement" would work and hoped to get Czech leaders to negotiate with the Germans. The United States, too, favored negotiations.

As the crisis progressed through the summer of 1938, Roosevelt gave some indication that he did not entirely share the views of the British prime minister. In conversations with the British ambassador, Sir Ronald Lindsay, he deplored Germany's brutal diplomacy, expressed the fear that, even if Czechoslovakia were to give in, new demands would be made on Poland, Rumania, and Denmark, and raised once again the possibility of a world conference. In a speech in Kingston, Ontario, on August 18, he also announced that the time had passed when controversies beyond the seas did not interest or harm the people of the Americas. But the United States continued to make clear throughout this period that it could not, in the event of war, supply either men or arms to the democracies. And it refused an appeal by Czechoslovakia for a statement of support on the grounds that the United States could not advise a nation to fight.

On the eve of the Munich conference, which was to seal the bargain Chamberlain had made with Hitler at Berchtesgaden and yield to all of the German dictator's demands in return for a paper promise of future good behavior, Roosevelt addressed two appeals to Hitler and one to Mussolini. He asked *Il Duce* to use his influence to arrange for a conference and the fuehrer to continue negotiations and to avoid war. But although he thereby played a modest role in the politics of Europe, he hastened to include in his second message to Germany the traditional American disclaimer: "The Government of the United States has no political involvements in Europe, and will assume no obligations in the conduct of the present negotiations."

Though Roosevelt had earlier described the settlement to be imposed on Czechoslovakia as "the most terrible, remorseless sacrifice" ever demanded of a country, he greeted the Munich agreement with a sense of relief that peace had been preserved. That sentiment was shared by Hull and by most other State Department officials. But the enormity of what had been done to Czechoslovakia—ironically to the most democratic state to have been created by the Versailles Treaty—and the arrogance of Germany (which was only fed by this new triumph) produced sober second thoughts. Within a month of the agreement, Roosevelt was warning the American people that "peace by fear has no higher or more enduring quality than peace by the sword." By early November, after the so-called Crystal Night, when synagogues throughout Germany had been put to the torch and Jewish businesses smashed by uniformed hoodlums, and when Jewish adult males had been sent temporarily to concentration camps and a billion mark fine assessed against the German Jewish community, the United States for the first time gave clear and unmistakable evidence of its disapproval of German policy. "The people of the United States," the Foreign Relations Committee chairman, Key Pittman, declared in an extraordinary public statement, "do not like the Government of Germany." And Roosevelt himself said at a press conference that he "could scarcely believe that such things could occur in a twentieth century civilization." On November 15, 1938, the United States recalled its ambassador in Berlin. He never returned to his post.

Public opinion in the United States now continued its transformation at an accelerating rate. While a survey taken in October 1937 had still found 62 per cent of Americans neutral in their attitude toward Germany, 56 per cent of those polled immediately after the Munich conference favored a boycott of German goods. That figure rose to 61 per cent after the Crystal Night. In his State of the Union message in January 1939, Roosevelt suggested that "there are many methods short of war, but stronger and more effective than mere words, of bringing home to aggressor governments the aggregate sentiments of our own people." A month later, 69 per cent of the respondents to a Gallup poll favored all aid to England short of war.

Whatever further proof was needed that Chamberlain had not brought "peace in our time" at Munich was provided by the German annexation of what remained of Czechoslovakia on March 14, 1939, and by Mussolini's invasion of Albania the following month. Neither of these actions could be defended on ethnic grounds nor considered as revisions of the Versailles settlement. Hitler, moreover, had clearly violated his solemn pledge, given only five months before, and the danger to all countries posed by the dictators now became too great to be ignored or combated by mere insulation. The State Department condemned both acts as "wanton lawlessness," and 66 per cent of Americans polled declared themselves prepared to supply Great Britain with arms and ammunition in case of war, despite the existence of neutrality legislation forbidding such action. On April 14, Roosevelt appealed to both Hitler and Mussolini, asking for concrete pledges that they would not attack thirty-one

Nazi anti-Semitism took several forms. The age-old charge of usury by "the eternal Jew" is the theme of the top poster. The one at right shows a wealthy Jew regarding world peace as "a pretty plaything."

An official of the Third Reich compels a Jew to sweep the sidewalk. The existence of a wealthy and successful Jewish community within Germany posed a problem for Nazi theories of racial superiority.

US Information Agency, National Archives

specified nations of Europe and the Middle East for at least ten years. His effort produced only derisive replies. Hitler told the Reichstag that he had polled the countries mentioned and that none felt the need for the guarantee suggested by Roosevelt. Mussolini declared that he would not be moved by "convivial vociferations, or Messiah-like messages."

With war in Europe now looming ever more clearly on the horizon, and with public sentiment in the United States rapidly shaking off its isolationist torpor, Roosevelt moved to lift at least some of the shackles which neutrality legislation had imposed on American policy. The cash-and-carry provision of the Neutrality Act of 1937 which related to war materials other than arms and ammunition was due to expire. The administration hoped, in effect, to eliminate the arms embargo by putting all trade with belligerents on a cash-and-carry basis. Senator Pittman introduced such legislation as "The Peace Act of 1939" and Roosevelt called congressional leaders to a White House conference to urge its passage. The effort failed. The House of Representatives amended the measure so as to restore the arms embargo, though it is noteworthy that 123 congressmen who had voted for the embargo in 1937 were now prepared to abandon it. In the Senate, the bill died in committee. Though a majority of the members of the Foreign Relations Committee favored repeal, two bitter political foes of the president joined the opponents of repeal in voting to postpone consideration. On August 5, 1939—less than a month before

Hitler's invasion of Poland began the Second World War—Congress adjourned without having taken any action, reassured perhaps by the statement of Senator William E. Borah that he had better sources than the State Department and that Europe was in no danger of war.

The role played by the United States during the 1930s was thus not a heroic one. Still strongly influenced by a tradition of nonentanglement and suspicion of the European powers, and weakened and turned further inward by the Great Depression, the United States neither moved effectively to check the militant dictators nor encouraged the other democracies to do so through collective action. Its policies proved to be those of drift which seemed to encourage and, at times, unwittingly to aid those who were clearly guilty of naked aggression.

But if the United States did little or nothing to preserve peace and world order, it did awaken toward the end of the period to the very real threat which a Europe dominated by totalitarian states would pose to its security and its traditional institutions. Under a president who was careful not to outrun public opinion, but who possessed the qualities of leadership necessary to alert the nation both to its danger and its duty, the United States came to recognize in these difficult times that the policies of the nineteenth century were ill-suited to meet the problems of the twentieth. When war once more engulfed the world in September 1939, therefore, America was able to move steadily and with surprising speed from nominal neutrality to effective commitment.

Chapter 5

AN END TO NEUTRALITY

The Neutrality Act of 1939 marked a decisive shift in American policy and paved the way for the flow of military assistance to the Allies. The rapid fall of Denmark, Norway, Holland, Belgium, and France by mid-1940 left Britain and the empire alone against Hitler's Germany and hastened America's retreat from neutrality. Now, obsolete arms and destroyers were provided to the British, and the Lend-Lease bill won approval in Congress. Rearmament went ahead quickly, and peacetime conscription was introduced. Although the United States was still officially neutral, Roosevelt had led the nation a considerable distance along the road to aiding the Allied cause.

Reacting to War in Europe

On August 23, 1939, a nonaggression pact between Nazi Germany and Soviet Russia was made in Moscow. This astonishing diplomatic event was a clear sign of the imminence of war in Europe. And at dawn on September 1, without any formal warning, Germany invaded Poland. Two days later Britain and France declared war on Germany. The Second World War had begun.

On September 5, President Roosevelt issued a Proclamation of Neutrality, closely following the precedent of President Wilson's proclamation of August 4, 1914—but with one very significant difference. Wilson had followed his proclamation with an appeal to his fellow countrymen who were, as he said, "drawn from many nations, and chiefly from the nations now at war." He had declared: "The United States must be neutral in fact as well as in name during these days that are to try men's souls. We must be impartial in thought as well as in action." Twenty-five years later, Roosevelt, in the preamble of his proclamation, asserted: "The laws and treaties of the United States, *without interfering with the free expression of opinion and sympathy* [author's italics], nevertheless impose upon all persons . . . the duty of an impartial neutrality during the existence of the contest."

Even before the proclamation, in a "fireside chat" on the radio on September 3, he had made the same point. His words are worth quoting at some length because they also pose, at the very outset of the European war, the whole dilemma which would dominate the foreign policy of the United States for the next two years.

It is easy for you and me, to shrug our shoulders and to say that conflicts taking place thousands of miles from the whole American Hemisphere do not seriously affect the Americas—and that all the United States has to do is to ignore them and go about its own business. Passionately though we may desire detachment, we are forced to realize that every word that comes through the air, every ship that sails the sea, every battle that is fought, does affect the American future. . . . Let no man or woman thoughtlessly or falsely talk of America sending its armies to European fields. . . . This nation will remain a neutral nation, but I cannot ask that every American remain neutral in thought as well. Even a neutral has a right to take account of facts. Even a neutral cannot be asked to close his mind or his conscience. I have said not once, but many times, that I have seen war and that I hate war. I say that again and again. I hope the United States will keep out of this war. I believe that it will. And I give you assurance and reassurance that every effort of your Government will be directed toward that end.

There can be little doubt that this view coincided with that of the mass of Americans at the time. Popular opinion, as revealed in the opinion polls, was determined to maintain American neutrality. But it was much more strongly anti-German than it seems to have been in 1914. One poll in October 1939 showed that, although 99 per cent of the American people favored neutrality, only 2 per cent were pro-German as compared with 84 per cent who favored the Allies. American mistrust of Hitler's arbitrary rule and the Nazi persecution of the Jews had seen to that.

Already, however, the facts of wartime life were beginning to impinge, as Roosevelt had foreseen they would, upon the United States. On September 8, he proclaimed a state of limited national emergency in order to preserve American neutrality. The powerful magnetic field set up by the German conflict had begun to exercise its increasing pull upon America, as the earlier war had done a quarter of a century before.

One immediate problem facing the administration was that a vital section of the neutrality acts—prohibiting the export of certain raw materials to belligerents, except in American vessels and unless they had first been paid for in cash (the so-called cash-and-carry clause)—had expired on May 1. Furthermore, Roosevelt's private view, shared by some of his colleagues, was that the defeat of the Allies would result in a grave threat to the security of the United States—yet the export of war materials to the Allies, who badly needed them, was still forbidden by the neutrality laws.

He accordingly called Congress into special session on September 21 to amend the neutrality legislation by "a return to international law." Six weeks of bitter debate followed, but on November 4 the president signed the new Fourth Neutrality Act. It was in effect a compromise between the isolationists and those who felt the need to give economic support to Britain and France. The embargo on the export of arms was repealed, but cash and carry was imposed on all war materials. Prohibition of travel by Americans on the vessels of belligerents and of American loans to nations at war were retained. A new provision excluded American ships altogether from certain "combat zones," which were to be defined by presidential proclamation.

Despite these restrictions, the new legislation was a most important Allied victory. It made possible an increasingly formidable flow of American-produced arms and munitions to France and Britain, while Allied sea power prevented almost entirely United States exports to Germany. During the first year of the war, 44 per cent of all American exports went to the British Empire, but cash and carry soon began to throw a severe strain on Allied dollar resources. Certain provisions of the neutrality law did, however, reduce friction over neutral maritime rights, not only with Britain (which the administration

UPI

did all in its power to ease) but also with Germany. Finally, as had happened in 1914, war (once described by the English reformer Richard Cobden as "the great consumer") did what the New Deal had really failed to do—it began to cure America's economic depression.

Meanwhile, the strangest period of the war in Europe ensued. The Luftwaffe's bombing of Warsaw, and the German army's *Blitzkrieg* towards the capital from the west, were aided and abetted on September 17 by Russia's invasion of Poland from the east, under a secret treaty signed at the time of the nonaggression pact. The military subjugation of the Polish people was soon complete and yet another German-Russian partition of Poland became a part of history. On the Western Front, including the "impregnable" French Maginot Line, activity was minimal. No strategic air bombing took place, except the dropping of propaganda leaflets. The naval blockade was in operation but could only bite slowly, if at all, with Germany's whole eastern frontier at peace. The period of the "phony war" had begun, and an unnatural quiet settled over a Europe technically at war.

Except in one bizarre theater of operations. As well as invading Poland, Stalin had established control over the three tiny Baltic republics of Lithuania, Latvia, and Estonia which had been set up after the First World War. He followed this with a demand that Finland should cede to Russia certain territory which Moscow regarded as vital to the defense of Leningrad. The Finns appealed to the United States. President Roosevelt tendered his good offices to Stalin, only to have them rejected. On November 30 (in the current fashion, without a declaration of war) Russia attacked Finland.

For a complex of reasons—including the extreme toughness of the Finns, the relatively confined area of crucial operations (in which Russian strength, especially in armor, could not be fully deployed), and the combination of Russian strategic overconfidence with the low morale of the Red Army after Stalin's prewar purges— Finland held her giant enemy at bay for more than three months. She got a great deal of American, as well as

Soviet Foreign Minister V. M. Molotov signs for Russia the nonaggression pact made with Germany in 1939. Directly behind him stand Joachim von Ribbentrop (left) and Joseph Stalin.

The Nazi invasion of Poland brought war to Europe. Left: The Luftwaffe as portrayed by a Polish artist: the death machines wreak havoc on land that refuses to succumb. Right: The Germans enter Danzig.

British, moral support (especially because she was the only European power that paid its American war debts, being the only one with a substantial favorable trade balance with the US). But Finland received no American military assistance. Britain, in one of her wilder flights of political fantasy, organized a volunteer force of skiing experts to go to the military aid of Finland. But it never took the field, since Finland accepted Russia's terms on March 12, 1940.

The Winter War was a strange interlude, but one which cast shadows into the postwar world. The Soviet Union's purposes now seem plain. Deeply skeptical about capitalist motives, Stalin hoped that he could buy off Hitler. But he was determined to exact as the price a strategic and military buffer zone between the homelands of the Soviet Union and those Western nations, especially Germany, which had in the past so frequently invaded the Russian Motherland. It was to stretch from Finland to the Black Sea, including the province of Bessarabia (and if possible Bukovina) in Rumania, both of which Russia ultimately seized in the summer of 1940. The dramatic advances made by Russia in these years can be seen basically as the natural, if deplorable, surge of German and Russian power back into the political vacuum of inadequate "liberal" regimes created in Eastern Europe by the Russian and German defeats in 1917–18 and the subsequent withdrawal from Europe of the dominant power of the Versailles peace table, the United States of America.

Hitler's motives, too, are clear. He wished to buy time to defeat France (and possibly Britain) in the West, in order to avoid the war on two fronts which he had always professed so much to dread. Each dictator believed that he had outsmarted the other. In the short term Hitler was right, but in the long term he was devastatingly wrong.

Blitzkrieg in the West

The "phony war," however, was not to last long. France and Britain had refused to come to terms when Hitler approached them soon after the consolidation of his conquest of Poland, which the Allies would have had to recognize. On April 9, Nazi forces attacked and rapidly occupied Denmark and Norway. Then, while the Allies were adjusting awkwardly to this relatively peripheral military development, Hitler turned the whole might of his new German military machine against the West. On May 10, in a massive sudden attack by land and air, the Netherlands, Belgium, and Luxembourg were attacked. And the inactive French front burst now into flame under the impact of the German onslaught.

Holland capitulated within five days, Belgium within eighteen. France surrendered on June 22, when a "rump" of the French state, the so-called Vichy regime of Marshal Pétain, signed an armistice agreement in the very same railroad carriage in the forest of Compiègne in which Marshal Foch had received the surrender of the German forces in 1918. The new French government, still in control of North Africa and a truncated metropolitan territory with direct access to the sea only on the Mediterranean, became neutral. Exiled governments from most of the conquered states of Europe fled to London, and a little known French general, Charles de Gaulle, set up the Free French movement there. In effect, however, Britain, albeit with the empire and Commonwealth, stood alone.

On June 10, when the overwhelming extent of the German victory had become apparent, Mussolini declared war on France and Britain. He sent troops over the Italian

*The Nazis launched their attack against
Norway in April 1940, and two months later had
ended internal resistance and repelled the
Allies at sea. The conquest of tiny Holland
was even swifter. Five days after the Germans
swept west on May 10, the Dutch surrendered.
Below: German paratroopers land
in Norway. Right: A German ski patrol in
the north of the country. Bottom: A German
destroyer in Norwegian waters. Opposite:
Paratroopers drift down over Holland on the
morning of May 10, the first day of the German
offensive against the Low Countries.*

Hugo Jaegar Life © Time Inc. 1975

In May and June 1940,
the German war machine
carried all before it.
Above: Soldiers of the
Third Reich in subdued
Belgium. Right: Troops
pass through the ruins of
a devastated town in
northern France. The fall
of the republic in June
left Britain and her empire
to face Germany alone.

AP

Imperial War Museum

Although it had a heroic side, the evacuation of 300,000 troops from Dunkirk in France testified to Germany's military supremacy in Europe. C. Cundall's oil portrays the retreat under heavy German air fire.

Alps to invade the south of France. This act, which was to earn the Italian dictator Winston Churchill's description of "the jackal," was deeply repugnant also to Roosevelt. That very day the president was due to make a speech at the University of Virginia in Charlottesville. He described his efforts to encourage Italian neutrality, and then said:

The Government of Italy has now chosen to preserve what it terms its "freedom of action" and to fulfill what it states are its promises to Germany. In so doing it has manifested disregard for the rights and security of other nations, disregard for the lives of the peoples of those nations which are directly threatened by this spread of the war; and has evidenced its unwillingness to find the means through pacific negotiations for the satisfaction of what it believes are its legitimate aspirations.

It was a hot day, but the president's complaints about the heat on the hundred-mile journey from Washington probably owed as much to his welling sense of indignation at Italy's action, as to the heat itself. He had been turning over in his mind, and probably discussed with one of his advisers, Sumner Welles, under-secretary of state (who advised against it), the inclusion of a sharply condemnatory note in his speech. In the event, perhaps on the spur of the moment, he continued: "On this tenth day of June 1940, the hand that held the dagger has struck it into the back of its neighbor." Benito Mussolini had been neatly placed in his historical niche.

Roosevelt had already reacted sharply and profoundly to the prospective fall of France. One-time assistant secretary of the navy, and disciple of Admiral Mahan, he knew by now that the whole Atlantic coastline of continental Europe from Norway to the neutral Iberian Peninsula was going to be in the hands of Hitler and his navy and air force. Britain's hold on the Mediterranean, and perhaps the whole Middle East beyond it, would accordingly be gravely challenged. He was not to know that a month later, on July 3, the British were, as far as possible, to seize or sink, in French ports, the major vessels of the French navy (now in Vichy hands), following what Churchill was to call a "hateful decision" by the British government, but one that was perhaps a better gauge of Britain's desperate situation than any other.

The military and political upheaval of these three early summer months of 1940 was probably the greatest international earthquake since Napoleonic times. It was profoundly to affect the attitude of the people of the United States to the war. Even more decisively than

107

Keystone

When a benefit party was held in New York for
French relief in October 1940, pickets protested
that such aid would assist the Germans.

before, Roosevelt took the lead in educating the American public to the cataclysmic pace of developments. The whole tone and content of his Charlottesville speech contrast markedly with his fireside chat at the beginning of the conflict. Now he declared:

Perception of danger, danger to our institutions, may come slowly or it may come with a rush and a shock as it has to the people of the United States in the past few months. . . . Some indeed still hold to the now somewhat obvious delusion that we of the United States can safely permit the United States to become a lone island, a lone island in a world dominated by the philosophy of force. Such an island may be the dream of those who still talk and vote as isolationists. Such an island represents to me and to the overwhelming majority of Americans today a helpless nightmare, the helpless nightmare of a people without freedom; yes, the nightmare of a people lodged in prison, handcuffed, hungry, and fed through the bars from day to day by the contemptuous unpitying masters of other continents. . . . Let us not hesitate—all of us—to proclaim certain truths. Overwhelmingly we, as a Nation . . . are convinced that military and naval victory for the gods of force and hate would endanger the institutions of democracy in the western world, and that equally, therefore, the whole of our sympathies lies with those nations that are giving their life blood in combat against these forces. . . . In our American unity, we will pursue two obvious and simultaneous courses; we will extend to the opponents of force the material resources of this Nation and, at the same time, we will harness and speed up the use of those resources in order that we ourselves in the Americas may have equipment and training equal to the task of any emergency and every defense.

Pressure groups rapidly sprang up in the United States to push their particular points of view. The Committee to Defend America by Aiding the Allies, headed by the Kansas journalist William Allen White, was founded on May 19 and had 600 branches in less than two months. Within it an eastern ginger faction favored outright intervention, including war if necessary. The main opposing group was the isolationist America First Committee, in which the aviator hero Charles A. Lindbergh played a leading role. But it suffered from the support of such pro-Nazi organizations as the German-American Bund.

Although American opinion ran strongly in favor of the Allies, isolationist groups conducted persuasive campaigns against entering the war. These posters were issued by the America First Committee, which continued to lobby Congress as late as 1941.

The German-American Bund

Several American organizations embraced aspects of Nazi philosophy in the 1930s, among them the Silver Shirts, the Defenders of the Christian Faith, and the Knights of the White Camellia. But the most significant and best-known Fascist body in the United States before the Second World War was the German-American Bund.

It was founded after a public meeting in Buffalo, New York, in March 1936. Earlier Nazi groups had incurred the displeasure of Germany, but now Fritz Kuhn emerged as leader of the new movement.

For the next three years the bund attracted a good deal of public attention —and apprehension. At meetings and rallies the swastika hung next to the Stars and Stripes; uniformed members sang patriotic German and American songs; and, although both languages were used, official party directives were written in German. Local branches could operate in secret, and members sometimes assumed fictitious names on joining.

The bund held camps for the children of German families, the most important of which were Camp Siegfried on Long Island and Camp Nordland near Andover in New Jersey. There also, the faithful gathered for mass rallies. In 1941 a magazine reported how, on such occasions, "members of the Bund do the goosestep and drill in military formations, digest endless propaganda talks, papers and films, and learn to hate Catholics, Jews, Negroes and Communists." In St Louis, where people of German extraction made up 12 per cent of the population, the bund held summer classes for study of the German language.

Aryan blood was an essential prerequisite of membership. Kuhn informed branches that the bund "is conducted upon the Fuehrer principle. Consequently there are no elections, no majority decisions." Close links were established with the Reich: members undertook intelligence work for Berlin and helped distribute Nazi propaganda. Kuhn led a delegation to Germany in 1936 and met Hitler. The bund also published its own newspapers in several major cities, including New York, Los Angeles, and Chicago. Its main aim was to "defend the old Fatherland against agitation and slander."

At a time of mounting tension in Europe, the bund aroused concern in the United States. Indeed, the German ambassador reported to Berlin in 1937 that its activities were counterproductive: "Instead of arousing sympathetic understanding of the German cause among the masses, they engender antagonism."

Many records of the bund were later destroyed, but in 1937 the Justice Department estimated membership at under 7,000, although Kuhn claimed 25,000 adherents. Certainly the largest rally ever held by the bund, to celebrate George Washington's birthday, attracted 20,000 to Madison Square Garden in 1939.

From 1937 the House of Representatives began investigating subversion in the United States, and the German-American Bund came under official scrutiny. Furthermore, in May 1939 Kuhn was arrested on charges of embezzling bund money. By the end of that year he was serving a jail sentence.

Now thoroughly discredited, the bund was in retreat. With the outbreak of war in Europe, and American sentiment running strongly against Germany, membership of the bund ebbed away. The movement lingered on for a number of years before fading quietly into history.

Below: Loyalty to the Fatherland was strong among German immigrants. This reunion took place in 1937. Opposite: Fritz Kuhn at a bund rally.

Churchill Comes to Power in Britain

The immediate question was that of military aid to Britain. The principal (and most compelling) argument advanced against it by the isolationists was that military equipment sent to the United Kingdom would only be lost to the United States when, as seemed to them inevitable, Britain herself shortly succumbed to Germany. Neville Chamberlain, indelibly associated in the American mind with the policy of appeasement, and not a war leader by nature, had stayed on as prime minister until the attack on the West in the spring. The American ambassador in London, Joseph P. Kennedy, was personally sympathetic to Chamberlain, largely because he was himself a convinced supporter of the appeasement policy. He had not inspired American opinion with confidence in Britain's will to win. A *Fortune* poll at this time showed that only 30 per cent of Americans were still confident of an Allied victory. Some 63 per cent believed that Hitler would try to seize territory on the American side of the Atlantic.

Happily, Chamberlain resigned on the very day of the German offensive, May 10, and was succeeded by a very different sort of man. In his first speech to the House of Commons on May 13, Winston Churchill declared that he had nothing to offer but "blood, toil, tears and sweat" and a determination "to wage war by sea, land and air, with all our might and with all the strength that God can give us." These words, of course, were for the British people, a call to them to "stiffen the sinews, summon up the blood." Churchill once claimed only "to give expression to the opinion of the people of this country, and I was fortunate in being able to put their sentiments into words." As Lord Strang, a former Foreign Office

Joseph P. Kennedy with part of his family in London. Ambassador to Britain from 1937 until 1940 when he resigned, Kennedy doubted whether Britain could withstand Germany, and advised against US involvement.

UPI

official, wrote: "Never was a people more nobly mirrored to itself."

The eye of this master propagandist, however, was never entirely off the effect of his words on a wider constituency—the whole English-speaking world, and above all the United States. He showed a deep, even instinctive, understanding of the American people. Not surprisingly, for as he was to write later, "American blood flowed in my veins." Even in perhaps the most famous of his speeches, on June 4, 1940, he was concerned not only to fortify the resolution of the British people, but also to make it crystal clear to the Americans that Britain was worth supporting and would not succumb to the Nazi onslaught.

> Even though large tracts of Europe and many old and famous states have fallen or may fall into the grip of the Gestapo and all the odious apparatus of Nazi rule, we shall not flag or fail. We shall go on to the end. We shall fight in France, we shall fight in the seas and oceans, we shall fight with growing confidence and growing strength in the air; we shall defend our Island, whatever the cost may be. We shall fight on the beaches, we shall fight on the landing-grounds, we shall fight in the fields and in the streets, we shall fight in the hills; we shall never surrender.

And then he continued, in a matchless passage, not only to evoke deep British memories but to indicate subtly the moral of it all for the great American Republic:

> . . . and even if, which I do not for a moment believe, this Island or a large part of it were subjugated and starving, then our Empire beyond the seas, armed and guarded by the British Fleet, would carry on the struggle, until, in God's good time, the New World, with all its power and might, steps forth to the rescue and liberation of the Old.

As he wrote later, "After the collapse of France the question . . . arose in the minds of all our friends . . . 'Will Britain surrender too?' . . . I had repeatedly declared our resolve to fight on alone. After Dunkirk . . . I had used the expression 'if necessary for years, *if necessary alone.'* This was not inserted without design."

Not that he ever allowed himself or the British people to be lulled, if there was any danger of it, into a false sense of security by the magic of his oratory. He had seen too much of that in the 1930s, not only in an appeasing Britain, but above all in an isolationist United States. The belief that America, already the most powerful nation in history, could isolate herself permanently from the rest of the world, especially a world with Adolf Hitler at large in it, contained a large element of fantasy. The fall of France represented, as Roosevelt himself noted, the sudden and brutal intrusion of reality into this fantasy world. Churchill never allowed the United States to slip back into unreality unchecked. As he wrote to the British ambassador in Washington on June 28, "Too much attention should not be paid to eddies of United States opinion. Only force of events can govern them. Up till April they were so sure the Allies would win that they did not think help necessary. Now they are so sure we shall lose that they do not think it possible." Never cease to impress on the president, he instructed the ambassador, that if a Quisling government surrendered the American fleet to Germany, "Feeling in England against United States would be similar to French bitterness against us now. We have really not had any help worth speaking of from the United States so far. We know the President is our best friend, but it is no use trying to dance attendance upon Republican and Democratic Conventions. What really matters is whether Hitler is master of Britain in three months or not." Churchill's feet were always planted firmly on the earth.

Even in his descriptions of the evacuation of the great bulk of the British Expeditionary Force from Dunkirk—"a miracle of deliverance, achieved by valor, by perseverance, by perfect discipline, by faultless service, by resource, by skill, by unconquerable fidelity"—he never varnished the truth. This army of 300,000 had to come back, after all, without its guns, even without its small arms, and he called it what it was, "A colossal military disaster." On the other hand, he did not fail to point out, directly or by implication, the advantages which Britain did still have—the effective victory of the fighters of the Royal Air Force, the British Navy, the island position of Britain. Largely as a result of appeals to Roosevelt, very soon after Churchill became prime minister, the United States administration did begin to aid Britain directly and on an increasing scale.

Military Support for Britain

Despite isolationist opposition, means were found to circumvent the neutrality laws and American obligations under international law. Under an old act of 1917, "obsolete" government war materials were turned over to private manufacturers who could then transfer them to Britain. About 150 planes were made available during June, and 600,000 Lee-Enfield rifles, 800 French and British 75 mm guns, and 80,000 machine guns, with considerable quantities of ammunition, followed in July.

These were not released by the American services out of a bountiful supply. As General George Marshall, army chief of staff, said to Henry Morgenthau, Jr, secretary of the Treasury, and one of the most energetic and effective advocates of aid to Britain, "Our situation in bombers is very serious . . . because we have this antiquated force. . . . The shortage is terrible, and we have no ammunition for anti-aircraft and will not for six months. . . . Anti-tank guns, the situation is similar, a shortage. .50 caliber, our situation is the same." In this conversation, recorded by Morgenthau in his *Diaries*, Marshall also said, "We have ignored the legal requirements, both of the Neutrality Act and of the law which states exactly how we will declare things surplus and we have ignored the political implications of any action. We have addressed ourselves simply to the proposition, duly safeguarding our situation of national defense . . . of . . . what . . . might we spare if means were found of getting it over to the Allies." Asked Morgenthau: "How's your conscience on this?"

Those in the administration who could square it with their consciences, who favored the bold course of helping Britain to the utmost, were not yet wholly in control of policy. But on June 19 when the president asked for the resignation of Secretary of War Harry Woodring, a convinced isolationist who had long been at loggerheads with his own assistant secretary, Louis Johnson, as well as with the other interventionists in the administration, a decisive step was taken in that direction. Exactly how decisive only became clear when Roosevelt appointed as Woodring's successor Henry L. Stimson, and at the same time made Frank Knox, also a Republican, secretary of the navy. Both men were not only of vigor and experience but of pronounced pro-Allied views. Both had recently called for strong measures, including rapid naval rearmament and compulsory national military training, which had never before existed in peacetime in the United States.

The president and the main officers of the administration were in fact moving towards the position of American non-belligerency (that is, of giving all aid short of war). Churchill had asked this of Roosevelt on May 15 in his very first telegram to the White House after becoming prime minister. The speed of political change, dictated by the headlong rush of military events (with which indeed it seemed quite unable to keep pace), had outrun legal niceties. Roosevelt could not proclaim such a position openly, but he did all he could to force the pace. He had, since the beginning of the war, been in regular personal correspondence with Churchill. This close relationship was maintained and subsequently strengthened by a growing personal cordiality.

The president had not been able to accede to certain further requests which were made by the prime minister in this remarkable keynote document of May 15. He had also asked, among other things, for a range of raw materials as well as weapons; for a visit by the United States Navy to Irish ports; for a strong American line in the Pacific (using Singapore if needful); and had even foreshadowed the problem of the British need for dollars in view of the cash and carry policy. But the "hardest" request, in both senses of the word, was for the loan of forty or fifty old American destroyers, then in "mothballs" in American dockyards. This was not just a shopping list, but a sort of tentative yet prophetic blue-print of a policy

The appointment in 1940 of Henry L. Stimson (left) as secretary of war and Frank Knox as secretary of the navy affirmed FDR's desire to aid Britain as much as possible. Both men wanted naval rearmament and compulsory military training.

for the United States over the next twelve months or so.

The demand for destroyers was the crucial one, for Britain depended above all on control of the seas. Moreover, she had lost the use of most of the French Navy at a time when her needs were hugely multiplied by the numerous new bases available to the German U-boats along the now seemingly endless coastline of Europe. At first the request for the vessels was refused. But the idea persisted, and Churchill persisted too. On May 20, five days after his initial telegram, he returned to the matter in another masterly document:

Our intention is, whatever happens, to fight on to the end in this Island, and, provided we can get the help for which we ask, we hope to run them [the Germans] very close in the air battles in view of individual superiority. Members of the present Administration would [be] likely [to] go down during this process should it result adversely, but in no conceivable circumstances will we consent to surrender. If members of the present Administration were finished and others came in to parley amid the ruins, you must not be blind to the fact that the sole remaining bargaining counter with Germany would be the Fleet, and if this country was left by the United States to its fate no one would have the right to blame those then responsible if they made the best terms they could for the surviving inhabitants. Excuse me, Mr President, putting this nightmare bluntly. Evidently I could not answer for my successors, who in utter despair and helplessness might well have to accommodate themselves to the German will. However, there is happily no need at present to dwell upon such ideas.

He did not confine himself to secret diplomacy, but used his public utterances to bring the issues home to the

American people. On June 18 in a great parliamentary oration he declared:

> What General Weygand called the Battle of France is over. I expect that the Battle of Britain is about to begin. Upon this battle depends the survival of Christian civilization. . . . Hitler knows that he will have to break us in this Island or lose the war. If we can stand up to him, all Europe may be free and the life of the world may move forward into broad, sunlit uplands. But if we fail, then the whole world, including the United States, including all that we have known or cared for, will sink into the abyss of a new Dark Age, made more sinister, and perhaps more protracted, by the lights of perverted science. Let us therefore brace ourselves to our duties, and so bear ourselves that, if the British Empire and its Commonwealth last for a thousand years, men will still say: ''This was their finest hour.''

Meanwhile, he maintained the diplomatic pressure for the destroyers at a number of levels. This was perhaps most effectively pursued (with the frankly defeatist Kennedy still ambassador in London) through Arthur Purvis, head of the now British-dominated Anglo-French Purchasing Mission in Washington, and Secretary of the Treasury Morgenthau. But even now the best argument was neither speeches nor diplomacy but the progress of the war. On August 5 the Anglo-German air war flared up into the decisive Battle of Britain, which formed the background to the crucial negotiations. These were in fact completed before the battle was obviously won in mid-September, when it also became clear that the German invasion of Britain would not take place, at least for the present. (It is now known that Germany's Operation Sea Lion was indefinitely postponed on September 17.)

The main obstacles raised by opponents of the deal were that it was contrary not only to the Neutrality Act but to international law, and that it would involve the United States in war on the side of a possibly, even probably, beaten Britain. The Chicago *Tribune*, mouthpiece of isolationism, wrote that ''the sale of the Navy's ships to a nation at war would be an act of war. If we want to get into war, the destroyers offer as good a way as any of accomplishing the purpose.'' There is little doubt that in traditional international law (and in American history the precedent of the *Alabama* claims after the Civil War wholly supported this view) it was a highly dubious act for a peaceful, neutral government. Churchill himself called it ''decidedly unneutral.'' But, as the Latin saying puts it, *inter arma silent leges*, ''laws are dumb in the midst of arms.''

Furthermore, even if transferred to private agencies for subsequent sale, the transaction was plainly contrary to the Neutrality Acts—unless the goods were paid for in cash, which would require an enormous sum in dollars. The breakthrough occurred with an American suggestion in early August that Britain might trade certain British

The course of the war in Europe nudged American policy away from neutrality in 1940. The Battle of Britain added weight to Churchill's requests for American military aid. Right: An outdated destroyer arrives in Britain as part of a destroyers-for-bases swap.

Keystone

bases in the Western Hemisphere for the destroyers. Ninety-nine-year leases on six British bases in the Bahamas, Jamaica, Antigua, St Lucia, Trinidad, and British Guiana were accordingly exchanged for fifty over-age American destroyers. Two other leases, the most important, in Bermuda and Newfoundland, were given as free gifts, to assuage the pride of those Britons who might resent, as Churchill put it, this "naked trading away of British possessions."

This enabled Roosevelt to present the whole transaction as in America's own strategic interest, which indeed it was. It was the one relatively immediate act of the United States which had a probably decisive effect on Britain's military situation. For its part, America received a formidable long-term defensive asset. Roosevelt was emboldened to agree to the deal, in the midst of the election campaign for his unprecedented third term, because his Republican opponent, Wendell Willkie, a thorough-going internationalist, took the issue of support for Britain out of the campaign. To the end, however, legal problems persisted. Roosevelt did not believe that a Congress in which isolationism was still strong would act with the speed which was militarily essential. As Churchill had written to him at the height of the negotiations, "I am sure you will not misunderstand me if I say that our willingness . . . must be conditional on our being assured that there is no delay." For his part, the prime minister formally assured the president that if "the waters surrounding the British Isles should become

untenable for British ships of war, a British Fleet would in no event be surrendered or sunk, but would be sent overseas for the defense of other parts of the Empire."

Only a few weeks earlier, Congress had inserted an amendment in a Naval Appropriation bill which forbade the dispatch of the destroyers unless the navy certified that they were useless for United States defense purposes. In the end Admiral Harold R. Stark, chief of naval operations, "privately certified that the exchange was essential to national defense." Publicly, Roosevelt handled the issue with his customary political skill, although, as his enemies pointed out, he displayed a lack of frankness. The agreement was finally signed on September 2, and Congress was notified the next day. Most Americans thought it a good bargain, but a hard core of isolationists remained unconvinced.

Rearmament and Lend-Lease

Far less controversial was the swift progress of America's own rearmament, which went rapidly ahead throughout the election campaign. On July 10 the president called on Congress for an army of 1,200,000 with equipment for a further 800,000; an increase in the air forces of 19,000 planes; and a navy big enough to meet any combination of powers. The cost of all this was unprecedented, nearly $4.85 billion. In fact, Congress voted over $5 billion.

Left: Lend-Lease had its opponents. Typical was the delegation from the Massachusetts Women's Political Club which presented a petition at the White House in February 1941 protesting the bill. It was felt that such a law could involve the United States in war. Right: Aircraft and war materials head across the Atlantic.

Even the president's cautious call for conscription on August 2, though it provoked an isolationist firework display, was not a contentious campaign issue, since Willkie was also in favor of it. And so the first peacetime Selective Service Act in American history was signed, admittedly after prolonged congressional debate, on September 16. Roosevelt was nevertheless deeply concerned during the campaign to disarm isolationist criticism. He made a number of statements which it was later to require all his ingenuity to explain away, such as the famous pledge that ''Your boys are not going to be sent into any foreign wars.'' In the event he decisively defeated Willkie, by 27 million to 22 million votes. Thus the world knew that, barring accidents, there would be in the White House for a further four years, a man who Churchill was to call later ''the greatest American friend we have ever known, and the greatest champion of freedom who has ever brought help and comfort from the new world to the old.''

Bringing ''help and comfort'' was proving more and more difficult in late 1940. Britain's supply of foreign currency, and of dollars in particular, was rapidly running out, despite the establishment of government control over all foreign assets held by Britons. Even if cash and carry had not existed, the shadow of bitterness over war debts in the interwar years would have remained. The matter was solved by perhaps the most inspired of FDR's political acts.

How was the United States to give the vital necessary help to Britain without violating (or repealing) the Johnson Act, which prohibited loans to governments in default on their First World War debts to America? In one of his most famous press conferences, Roosevelt discussed the matter in terms which the playwright, Robert E. Sherwood, believed ''won the fight for 'Lend-Lease'' there and then.''

> Now, what I am trying to do is to eliminate the dollar sign. That is something brand new in the thoughts of practically everybody in this room, I think—get rid of the silly, foolish old dollar sign. Well, let me give you an illustration: Suppose my neighbor's home catches fire, and I have a length of garden hose four or five hundred feet away. If he can take my garden hose and connect it up with his hydrant, I may help him to put out his fire. Now, what do I do? I don't say to him before that operation, ''Neighbor, my garden hose cost me $15; you have to pay me $15 for it!'' What is the transaction that goes on? I don't want $15—I want my garden hose back after the fire is over. . . . But suppose it gets smashed up . . . during the fire. . . . He says, ''All right, I will replace it!'' Now, if I get a nice garden hose back, I am in pretty good shape.

The congressional struggle was acrimonious none the less. The president's opponents, too, could evoke echoes

Peacetime conscription was introduced in the United States for the first time in 1940. Recruitment of volunteers was also stepped up (opposite). Isolationists protested the draft, but by this time they were out of step with majority opinion. Right: A New York rally by the isolationist America First Committee in May 1941 was attended by some of its best-known supporters. Shown on the platform are, from left: Senator Burton K. Wheeler, Charles A. Lindbergh, novelist Kathleen Norris, and socialist Norman Thomas.

of the past. Senator Burton K. Wheeler of Montana recalled the Agricultural Adjustment Administration's policies of ploughing in crops and slaughtering piglets. He called Lend-Lease the "New Deal's triple A foreign policy" of "ploughing under every fourth American boy." FDR called this "the most untruthful, the most dastardly unpatriotic thing that has been said in public life in my generation," adding "Quote me on that." On March 11, 1941, the bill, which had passed the Senate by 60 to 31 and the House by 317 to 71, was signed by the president.

The act was very widely drawn. It gave the president power, among other things, to lend or lease any defense article to any foreign country deemed vital to the defense of the United States, and even to communicate any American defense information to any such country. Now the highway was open to make the United States, with an agricultural and industrial might unprecedented in history, what Roosevelt called "the great arsenal of democracy."

Yet whatever the scale of the aid it could, even now, appear to some merely to give Britain a reprieve. Although the threat of invasion seemed to have diminished and the Battle of Britain had been won, steady German night bombing had now begun. Above all, the threat of strangulation through pressure on Britain's shipping lanes, principally by the U-boats, grew steadily more

formidable. The Lend-Lease Act forbade the convoying of belligerent vessels by American ships. Roosevelt took such steps as he felt were open to him to relieve pressure on the British Navy. But even at this point the chief of naval operations went much too fast and too far when he said, "The question as to our entry into the war now seems to be *when*, and not *whether*."

On April 10 the president extended the hemispheric neutrality zone, proclaimed by the American nations at Panama on October 2, 1939, far into the Atlantic— to longitude 25° west—including Greenland, which American troops shortly occupied by agreement with the Danish minister in Washington. This action had been in response to the German extension of their blockade area to include Iceland and Greenland's coastal waters on March 25, in retaliation for Iceland's declaration of its independence of imprisoned Denmark, and subsequent British occupation of the island. Roosevelt also ordered the navy to comb the area for Nazi vessels, and to broadcast their positions to British forces. He declared the Red Sea no longer a combat zone, thus opening this Middle East supply route via the Cape of Good Hope to American shipping supplying British forces there.

On May 21 an unarmed American merchant vessel the *Robin Moor*, carrying no contraband, was sunk in the South Atlantic by a U-boat in an area well clear of all

This German poster appeared after Hitler's June 1941 invasion of Russia. Stalin and Churchill are portrayed as lackeys of a gloating FDR who profits from their toil.

war zones declared by neutrals or belligerents, and the passengers were turned loose in lifeboats. It was the first torpedoing of an American ship. Germany then announced that all vessels carrying Lend-Lease equipment were liable to attack. Roosevelt at once, on May 27, went on the air and declared that "Our patrols are helping now to insure delivery of the needed supplies to Britain. All additional measures necessary to deliver the goods will be taken." He ended with a Proclamation of Unlimited National Emergency. This meant little in practice, but he had indeed brought the United States a long way from cash and carry.

At this point, as had happened before, the president seemed to hold back. He was always mindful, as Wilson had been before him, of the necessity of going to war only with a united American people behind him. It was a necessity heavily underlined by Wilson's ultimate repudiation by the country. At this time, mid-1941, a *Fortune* poll showed that 79.5 per cent of Americans believed that the United States was in the war for all practical purposes. But as late as September of the same year, 75 to 80 per cent were opposed to full and direct participation in the conflict. Determined as Roosevelt was never to outrun public opinion, Sherwood was justified in

writing, "Whatever the peril, he was not going to lead the country into war—he was going to wait to be pushed in."

But events soon resumed their onward march. On June 6 Congress passed a bill to take over and employ all foreign merchant ships immobilized in American ports. On June 14 all German and Italian assets in the United States were frozen. Arrangements were made in the greatest secrecy during June for the relief of British troops in Iceland by American forces, and the actual landing was made early the next month. During June, too, regular military and naval consultation began between Great Britain and the United States.

Then occurred one of the most decisive of all the events of the Second World War. On June 22, 1941, less than two years after the Nazi-Soviet nonaggression pact, Hitler attacked Russia on a 2,000-mile front. This changed the whole nature of the conflict from the American point of view. In the short term, the sudden defeat of Britain became much less likely; but in the long

Keystone

term, Japan was freed from fear of the Soviet Union if she chose to take more violent action in the Far East. Stalin had apparently ignored the warnings of both Churchill and Roosevelt. But the president had promised the prime minister to go along with the British in aiding Russia if she were attacked, on the Churchillian principle that if Hitler invaded Hell, Churchill would at least make a favorable reference to the Devil in Parliament.

The Roosevelt administration had recognized Soviet Russia for the first time in 1933. Although there was some American radical feeling for the Communist regime during the Great Depression, the predominant cast of the American mind was strongly anti-Communist. Many on the Right were not sorry to see nazism and communism tearing each other to pieces. At first, therefore, American aid to Russia was cautious, the more so because (as in the case of Britain a year before) it was thought unlikely that she could withstand the German onslaught. As her magnificent resistance continued and her sacrifices mounted, a genuine warmth towards the Russian people, if not the Soviet system, developed. In September the United States granted a credit of $100 million to Russia. This was shortly multiplied tenfold. The Soviet Union was also made eligible for Lend-Lease aid, which, after Pearl

The first meeting of Roosevelt and Churchill, off the Newfoundland coast, symbolized and affirmed a growing identity of interests. The Atlantic Charter that resulted boosted British morale.

Harbor, flowed as freely and as fast as very difficult supply lines and deep Soviet suspicions of all Western capitalist powers allowed.

The Atlantic Charter

Such suspicions, on the other hand, were minimal between Britain and America (at least by normal international standards). The shape of things to come was dramatized at this time by the first personal meeting in August 1941 of Roosevelt and Churchill. It was held in great secrecy at sea near Argentia, Newfoundland, on the cruiser *Augusta* and the battleship *Prince of Wales*. Here, in this fitting nautical setting, was laid the foundation of the confidential, almost intimate, relationship of the two leaders on which so much was to depend for the rest of the war. The American ambassador who had replaced

Kennedy in London, John G. Winant, records that on Churchill's return from this meeting "he stepped out of the car . . . and came across to shake hands, with the simple statement, 'I like your president.' He . . . liked him to the end."

The Newfoundland meeting had been at the suggestion of Roosevelt, and seems originally to have been intended to deal principally with politico-military matters. But it was almost a by-product of the conference which caught the imagination of the public—the declaration of principles which came to be known as the Atlantic Charter. This document was a broad and innocuous declaration of principles. Not unlike Wilson's Fourteen Points, it was necessarily more generalized and less specific—no aggrandizement by war, popular self-government, liberal economic and trade policies, freedom from fear and want (tall orders these), freedom of the seas, and "the establishment of a wider and permanent system of general security."

Bland though these points were, they represented a quite extraordinary announcement of what amounted to war aims by a non-belligerent, indeed still nominally neutral, power. Yet Churchill was not able to obtain much in the way of more positive American military action, except a valuable arrangement for the US Navy to convoy British as well as American ships in the North Atlantic. The meeting served at first to boost British morale, largely because it was widely, if wrongly, believed that America's prompt entry into the war had been arranged.

When time passed and this did not happen, there was considerable disillusion in Britain. Even Churchill wrote gloomily to Harry Hopkins towards the end of August, "I don't know what will happen if England is fighting alone when 1942 comes." Once more, however, events began to move forward. On September 4 the American destroyer *Greer*, when attacked by a German submarine while trailing it and announcing its position to British planes, retaliated with depth charges. Roosevelt seized the chance to announce in a radio speech on September 11 that "This was piracy. . . . The time for active defense is now. . . . From now on, if German or Italian vessels of war enter the waters the protection of which is necessary for American defense they do so at their own peril." This was the famous "shoot on sight" speech.

On October 9 the president asked Congress to revise the neutrality acts to allow the arming of merchant ships and, in effect, the entry of American vessels into belligerent ports. While the debate continued in Congress, the destroyer USS *Kearny* was attacked and eleven American lives were lost. On October 31 another American destroyer, the *Reuben James,* was sunk with the loss of 115 of her crew. Nevertheless, the revision of the neutrality legislation was only carried by relatively narrow margins in mid-November. That isolationism was far from dead was even more vividly illustrated

when, some weeks earlier, the vital extension of selective service had only passed the House by one vote.

As Sherwood, a close observer of the president, with full access to the Hopkins papers, wrote:

The truth was that as the world situation became more desperately critical, and as the limitless peril came closer and closer to the United States, isolationist sentiment became ever more strident . . . and Roosevelt was relatively powerless to combat it. He had said everything "short of war" that could be said. He had no more tricks left. The hat from which he had pulled so many rabbits was empty. The President of the United States was now the creature of circumstance which must be shaped not by his own will or his own ingenuity but by the unpredictable determination of his enemies.

This judgment came very much closer to the truth than that made at about the same time by Charles A. Beard in his 1948 history, *President Roosevelt and the Coming of the War 1941: A Study in Appearances and Realities.* In it, Beard virtually accused the dead president of systematically deceiving the American people in a conspiracy to involve the United States in the war without the assent of Congress. The dramatist's judgment was sounder in this case than that of the historian. FDR saw with the clarity of a great statesman and the courage of a cripple. On September 11, 1941, he said with force that "One peaceful nation after another has met disaster because each refused to look the Nazi danger squarely in the eye until it actually had them by the throat. The United States will not make that fatal mistake."

That it did not do so was in large part the result of Roosevelt's unremitting determination, before it was too late, to bring reality home to those Americans, many of them in Congress, who still lived in a static and sequestered fantasy society of nations—believing that America was remote from the wicked Old World their forbears had left for ever. In fact, of course, they lived in the world of *Mein Kampf* and the theory of the master race, of the airplane and atomic fission, of Buchenwald and Belsen.

In the event, the United States did *not* enter the war as a full belligerent before she was devastatingly attacked by Japan. And even then it was Germany and Italy that declared war on her. Roosevelt in December 1941 did not do very much more than Woodrow Wilson had done when he called upon Congress, on April 2, 1917, to "formally accept the status of belligerent which has thus been thrust upon it." From 1939 until 1941 Franklin D. Roosevelt at no point seems to have gone beyond his, and his countrymen's, accepted norms of diplomatic skill and political presentation of the facts. He faced up to his deep, indeed awesome, duty as America's president and commander in chief in an international scene that was changing with stupefying speed.

AP

The proximity of war was brought home dramatically by U-boat attacks on American merchant vessels. Left: Crew members inspect damage to the Kearny, torpedoed off Iceland in October 1941 with the loss of eleven lives. Below: Lashed to another vessel, the Kearny waits for repairs to be carried out in an Icelandic bay.

Navy Department, National Archives

Chapter 6

A DAY OF INFAMY

In 1940, Japan concluded a military alliance with Germany and Italy, and in the next two years its leaders planned the course that would lead to a new order in Asia. The United States tried to deflect them by trade embargoes and negotiation, but without success. Japan's hour of destiny was at hand: all that stood in the way was the mighty nation on the other side of the Pacific. So a plan was hatched to attack Pearl Harbor where the US Fleet was based. Washington was convinced that when Japan struck she would do so on her own doorstep—not thousands of miles from home. The very audacity of the assault would do much to make December 7, 1941, an unforgettable day in American history.

The Road to Pearl Harbor

Throughout the 1930s the United States viewed with growing resentment Japan's imperialist program. The seizure of Manchuria, the flouting of naval limitation, the attack on China proper, the sinking of the United States gunboat *Panay*, the closing of the Open Door in occupied China—all contributed to the developing estrangement. Finally in the summer of 1939, as the eyes of the world were focused on the rapidly deteriorating situation in Europe, the Roosevelt administration took its first significant action to restrain Japan. On July 26, 1939, Secretary of State Cordell Hull gave to Japan the required six-months notice bringing to an end the Japanese-American treaty of commerce of 1911. Once the treaty expired, the United States would be free to apply economic sanctions against Japan.

The treaty abrogation notice jolted the ministry of Premier Hiranuma Kiichiro in Tokyo. The following month the Japanese received an even greater jolt, and from an unexpected quarter. On August 23 the Nazi-Soviet nonaggression pact was announced. The Hiranuma ministry, which was at that very time negotiating with Germany for an anti-Soviet alliance, resigned in disgrace. For the next ten months Japan was governed by moderate cabinets, the first headed by General Nobuyuki Abe, the second by Admiral Mitsumasa Yonai. As German armies overran Poland in September, Japan pursued a cautious and uncertain policy. Washington also marked time, awaiting a clarification of the European struggle. When the treaty of commerce expired in January 1940, Hull informed the Japanese that though the United States would not conclude a new treaty, trade could continue on a day-to-day basis.

The German *Blitzkrieg* in Europe in the spring of 1940 inspired fears in Washington over possible Japanese designs on Southeast Asia. As the Netherlands fell to the Nazi juggernaut and the Dutch government fled to London, the United States expressed its concern to Japan over any possible change in the status quo in the oil-rich Netherlands East Indies. It turned out that American anxieties over the Indies were premature. Japan's immediate objective was to prosecute the China war rather than move southward. This became apparent as the Japanese sought to close the lines of supply to beleaguered China. When France fell in June, Japan forced the new Vichy regime to cut the flow of supplies through French Indochina and to allow the stationing of Japanese inspectors in Tonkin to ensure implementation of the arrangement. Japan also demanded that Britain close the Burma Road.

Stunned by the defeat of their army in France and knowing the weakness of their forces in the Far East, the British looked to the United States for counsel and support. On June 27 the British ambassador, Lord Lothian, asked Hull to lend support to a full settlement with Japan or join in resisting Japan either by imposing a full embargo on exports to Japan or by sending warships to Singapore; Lothian knew that both steps might result in war. Washington refused to go along with any of these proposals, and in the end the British settled upon a compromise policy. On July 14 the London government announced that the Burma Road would be closed for three months.

Other events of July 1940 were of far greater significance than the temporary closing of the Burma Road. Developments in both Japan and the United States put the two nations on a collision course. In Japan, Fumimaro Konoye returned to the premiership. Though not an extremist, Konoye had shown himself to be a pliable instrument of the military when he served as premier during 1937–38. Other appointments to the new cabinet indicated a swing of the pendulum toward extremism. The new foreign minister was the fiery Yosuke Matsuoka, who had headed the Japanese delegation that bolted the League of Nations in 1933. To the war ministry came

Appointed minister of war in mid-1940, Hideki Tojo personified Japan's policy of military expansion. Tojo became premier shortly before the attack on Pearl Harbor.

Black Star

Hideki Tojo. During the 1930s, Tojo had been a leading member of the Tosei-ha or "control faction" of militarists. Though opposing the violent methods of the Kodo-ha or "Imperial Way faction," which sought power through assassinations and coups, the control faction had the same objective—to gain political dominance and to achieve Japan's imperial destiny.

Within two weeks of its appointment, the new Japanese leadership adopted a program that would lead inexorably to war with the United States and Britain. The instrument of decision was the "liaison conference," which usually consisted of the premier, the foreign, war, and navy ministers, and the army and navy chiefs of staff. At meetings on July 19 and 27, this body formulated a policy document entitled "The Main Principles of Japan's Policy for Coping with the Situation in Accordance with World Developments." This program called for strengthening political solidarity with Germany and Italy. Troops and air bases were to be placed in French Indochina. Whether Japan would move farther into Southeast Asia would depend on developments in the war with China

"SCRAM!"

and on the course of the European war. Specifically, the policy stated that if the China Incident was settled, and the situation at home and abroad permitted, Japan would seize a favorable opportunity to resort to arms in the south. If domestic and foreign conditions developed in a peculiarly favorable way, Japan might use force in the southward advance even if still militarily committed in China.

The developments in Washington that coincided with the Japanese policy decision were not based upon knowledge of that program. They were founded rather upon a growing suspicion of Japan's aggressive designs and upon a new awareness of the scarcity of strategic materials. The first step came on July 2 when President Roosevelt signed "An Act to Expedite the Strengthening of National Defense." This legislation authorized the president to regulate by license or prohibit entirely the export of commodities essential to national defense. Which products would be restricted or embargoed at the outset was a subject of vigorous debate within the administration. Secretary of the Treasury Henry Morgenthau, Jr, first got

Library of Congress

US-Japanese relations chilled markedly in 1940. Above left: Donald Zec's cartoon comments on the ban placed on the export of aviation fuel, until then sold to Japan. Left: Officials sign the Tripartite Pact in Berlin. Japan had now openly sided with the Axis powers. Above: Joseph C. Grew, ambassador to Tokyo, warned the US of this step.

Roosevelt to agree to the embargoing of all oil and scrap metal. The final decision on July 26, however, stated that only aviation petroleum and number one grade scrap metal would be embargoed for the time being.

Hopes in Washington that the embargo step would give Japan pause were soon shown to be ill founded. In August Japan wrung from Vichy France an agreement permitting the setting up of air bases and the stationing of a limited number of troops in northern French Indochina. When Ambassador Joseph C. Grew in Tokyo learned that the Japanese were preparing to move into Indochina, he sent to Washington his "green light" telegram. For years Grew had urged Washington to be cautious and conciliatory, but he now told Hull that the time had arrived when a continuance of the use of patience and restraint would "tend to render relations between the United States and Japan increasingly uncertain." By the time Grew's telegram arrived, the Roosevelt administration had already come to the same conclusion. On September 19 the cabinet decided to embargo all scrap iron and steel. The next day Grew reported that Japan was about to sign an alliance with the Axis powers. Events followed in rapid succession. On the twenty-third, Japanese forces moved into northern Indochina. Two days later, America announced that scrap metal would be embargoed except for shipments to the British Empire. Finally, on the twenty-seventh, the Tripartite Pact was announced in Berlin.

Within a period of a few days, the United States and Japan had thus exchanged heavy blows. Henry L. Stimson, who had recently joined the cabinet as secretary of war, noted in his diary concerning the scrap metal embargo: "This is a direct hit at Japan, a point which I have hoped we would hit for a long time." The Tripartite Pact was directed just as pointedly at the United States. By its terms Germany, Italy, and Japan agreed to assist one another with all means when one of the three was attacked by a power not then involved in the European or the Sino-Japanese War. Agreements in force with Soviet Russia were not to be affected, a provision which left the United States as the obvious principal target. Other provisions recognized the leadership of Japan in establishing a new order in East Asia and the leadership of Germany and Italy in establishing a new order in Europe.

The Japanese move into northern Indochina and the conclusion of the Tripartite Pact ended British efforts at appeasement in Asia. On October 4, Winston Churchill informed Roosevelt that Britain would reopen the Burma Road at the end of the three month period on October 18, and he requested an American naval visit to Singapore. Roosevelt was glad to see the reopening of the Burma Road, but he turned down the request for American ships to visit Singapore. Since the spring of 1940, the United States Fleet had made its base at Pearl Harbor in the mid-Pacific, and Roosevelt resolved to keep it intact there. In October he gave brief consideration to reinforcing the

small Asiatic fleet in the Philippines, but he was dissuaded by Admiral William D. Leahy, who warned that only the least valuable ships should be sent because the Asiatic fleet might be lost in the event of war. Roosevelt decided at the same time not to withdraw the battleship fleet from Pearl Harbor to the West Coast of the United States, as was being recommended by the commander of the fleet, Admiral James O. Richardson. It was Richardson's belief that the fleet could be better prepared for war on the West Coast, but Roosevelt wanted it to remain at Pearl Harbor as a warning to Japan.

In the succeeding months the British continued efforts

The Pacific Fleet had the crucial task of defending American possessions in the Pacific area. On December 7, 1941, the warships at Pearl Harbor included eight battleships, nine cruisers, twenty-nine destroyers, and five submarines.

to get American ships at Singapore, but without success. When Anglo-American staff conferences were held in Washington from January to March 1941, the British asserted that Singapore was the key to their position in the East and asked that the United States assume some responsibility for its defense. This the United States refused to do. A compromise was nevertheless incorporated in the "ABC–1" plan that came out of the conferences. If Britain and the United States found themselves at war with both the Axis and Japan, the United States would strengthen its forces in the Atlantic and Mediterranean areas so that the British Commonwealth would be free to release the ships necessary to defend British territories in the Far East. In the Pacific, the United States Fleet's task was to be mainly defensive—the protection of American possessions in the Pacific—but it was also to undertake a diversion toward the Marshall and Caroline Islands to relieve pressure on Malaya.

The basic Anglo-American difference over Singapore persisted through the winter of 1940–41 and in the months thereafter. Though the United States was unwilling to meet the British wishes on this issue, it did take other measures designed to deter Japan. In December 1940 all iron and steel were put on the embargo list. In February 1941, a time when there were many rumors of an immi-

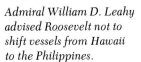

*Admiral William D. Leahy
advised Roosevelt not to
shift vessels from Hawaii
to the Philippines.*

*Harold R. Stark, chief of
naval operations, opposed
an embargo on oil exports
to Japan.*

*Ambassador Kichisaburo
Nomura took part in the talks
aimed at settling differences
between America and Japan.*

nent Japanese attack on Singapore, Eugene Dooman, counselor of the American embassy in Tokyo, gave the Japanese a stiff warning. In a conversation with the Japanese vice minister for foreign affairs, Chuichi Ohashi, Dooman said that if Japan were to prejudice the safety of British communications between the British Isles and the British Dominions and colonies overseas, either by direct action or by placing herself in a position to menace those communications, conflict with the United States could be expected. Dooman's warning was delivered without instructions from Washington, but it was not disavowed. On the contrary, Ambassador Grew reinforced it by giving the foreign minister, Matsuoka, a copy of the memorandum of the Dooman-Ohashi conversation. The following month the United States took another step to deter Japan: two cruisers and five destroyers were sent on a goodwill visit to Australia and New Zealand.

These steps had no discernible impact on Japan. Japanese naval leaders had serious doubts about the wisdom of the policy decision of July 1940, but the implementation of the program went ahead nevertheless. Returning to Tokyo from talks with German leaders in Berlin in April 1941, Matsuoka stopped in Moscow and negotiated a neutrality pact with Russia. It was apparent to Washington that Japan was attempting to secure the Manchurian flank in preparation for the southward advance. If the full story had been known, the news of the pact would have caused even more uneasiness. As early as February 1941, Ambassador Hiroshi Oshima told

the German foreign minister, Joachim von Ribbentrop, that preparations for the assault on Singapore would be completed by the end of May.

Other war plans were underway in Japan that not even Oshima knew about—plans for attacks on American territories. Japanese leaders assumed from the outset that war with Britain would automatically mean war with the United States. This calculation was justified, but it was an assessment that greatly worried Japanese navy leaders. They feared that Japan could not win a protracted war with the United States Navy. Even a short war would have grave risks unless the American fleet could be severely damaged at the outset. And so a plan to strike the United States Fleet at Hawaii was born.

It was Admiral Isoroku Yamamoto, commander in chief of the combined fleet, who proposed the attack on Pearl Harbor. Yamamoto was not enthusiastic about going to war with the United States, but he insisted that if Japan went to war with America, the Pearl Harbor attack must be included in the operations. Such an attack presented so many problems that it was a difficult task to solve them and convince other naval leaders of its feasibility. One obstacle was that Pearl Harbor was too shallow for existing aerial torpedoes. A further difficulty was created by Yamamoto's insistence that all six of Japan's large aircraft carriers be included in the task force. This would leave only three small carriers to support operations in the Philippines and elsewhere in Southeast Asia. Fashioning a shallow water torpedo was not achieved until early

November 1941, when the problem was solved by fixing special fins to regular torpedoes. The difficulty created by committing all large carriers to the task force was not solved until the same month, when the range of Zeros was extended sufficiently to permit the use of Formosa as a base for air attacks on the Philippines.

The sheer audacity of the Japanese plan to attack Pearl Harbor did much to assure its success. It was too much for American leaders, both in Washington and Hawaii, to credit. In January 1941, when Yamamoto was beginning to formulate the attack plan, Grew reported a rumor in Tokyo of such a plan. When the State Department relayed this information to the Office of Naval Intelligence, it was decided there that the rumor should be given no credence. This incident was only one of many during 1941 in which army and navy officers refused to take seriously the threat of a Japanese attack on Pearl Harbor.

However many failings can be justly charged to the army and navy during 1940–41, the armed services achieved one outstanding success—the Japanese diplomatic cipher was broken. Back in 1935, navy cryptologists had solved the mysteries of the Japanese top-secret cipher machine, which the Americans had called the "Red machine." Then in 1938 came a new challenge. Japan developed a more sophisticated cipher machine, labeled by American cryptologists the "Purple machine." The problem of breaking the new cipher was first tackled by a navy communications security unit under the command of Lieutenant Commander Lawrence F. Safford. By the end of 1938, Safford concluded that his staff had more work than it could handle. The task was turned over to an army signal intelligence service unit directed by Colonel William F. Friedman. In August 1940, in the nineteenth month of the effort, a major breakthrough occurred, and on September 25, 1940, the first ungarbled text was recovered.

The entire operation of intercepting, deciphering, and translating messages was given the name "Magic." The army and navy chiefs, General George C. Marshall and Admiral Harold R. Stark, were determined to guard closely the secret that the cipher had been cracked. During 1940 no Magic intercepts were allowed to leave the War and Navy Departments. In January 1941 the White House and the State Department were placed on the distribution list, but there was constant apprehension over lax security practices in those offices. Confidence in the White House was so lacking that only summarizing memos were sent there rather than the original intercepts. This caution was fully justified. Several times the memos were lost and then found in the unclassified wastepaper basket of Major General Edwin M. ("Pa") Watson, the president's genial military aide. The problem became so acute that, beginning in May 1941, only oral summaries were given to the White House. This practice continued until November 1941 when President Roosevelt insisted on getting texts of the Magic intercepts.

Security at the State Department was not much better. In April 1941 the entire operation was endangered when the under-secretary of state, Sumner Welles, revealed Magic intercept information to the Russian ambassador. Fortunately, when the Russians told the Germans and the Germans told the Japanese, the latter did not believe that the cipher had been cracked. Matsuoka believed, instead, the assurance given by the head of his cable section that it was "humanly impossible" to break the cipher. The system was thus secure, and it would remain so throughout the months of negotiations between Tokyo and Washington preceding the outbreak of war.

Attempts to Formulate an Agreement

The first steps toward the opening of Japanese-American talks had been taken at the beginning of 1941. Two Roman Catholic priests, Bishop James E. Walsh and Father James M. Drought, returned from Japan in January bringing a report that Matsuoka wished to improve relations with the United States. In Washington they sought out the postmaster general, Frank C. Walker, who took them to see Roosevelt and Hull. The following month there arrived in Washington a new Japanese ambassador, Admiral Kichisaburo Nomura, a man whom Hull later characterized as "honestly sincere in trying to avoid war." In March, informal meetings between Nomura and Hull began. Talks also went on at the Japanese embassy between Nomura, Walker, and the Catholic priests. From the embassy deliberations there emerged on April 9 the draft of a possible Japanese-American agreement.

The April 9 draft was comprehensive in scope. It dealt with all the major issues which were to appear and reappear in various forms during the months of informal talks which were to follow. By its terms each nation would pledge itself to use only peaceful means in the Southwest Pacific. Japan would agree not to go to war under the Tripartite Pact unless Germany or Italy were "aggressively" attacked. In return for these concessions, the United States would have to lift its embargo measures, help Japan get products from the Netherlands East Indies, recognize Manchukuo, and force Chiang Kai-shek to negotiate a settlement with Japan by withdrawing aid from China. The basis for the China settlement that was outlined in the draft left little to the imagination. The Chiang Kai-shek government and the Japanese-created Wang Ching-wei government were to "coalesce." The withdrawal of Japanese troops from China was to be worked out between Japan and China. This draft was not accepted by Hull, but he did assent to having it referred to Tokyo. With it he sent a statement of four principles, which he believed should be the guidelines in the drafting of an agreement: nondisturbance of the status quo in the Pacific except by peaceful means; noninterference in the internal affairs of other countries; observance of equal commercial opportunity; and respect for the territorial integrity of all nations.

Matsuoka found the April 9 draft awaiting him when he returned to Tokyo from his visit to Berlin and Moscow. Ecstatic over his talks with German leaders and his newly signed neutrality pact with Russia, he was in no mood for a Japanese-American agreement. He insisted that Washington must agree to a neutrality pact before the opening of negotiations for a comprehensive agreement. When Nomura presented the neutrality pact proposal, Hull promptly rejected it. If Matsuoka had had his way, there would have been no further efforts toward a Japanese-American agreement, but Premier Konoye, with the emperor's support, overruled the foreign minister. Consequently, on May 12 a Japanese draft for an agreement was submitted to Hull by Nomura. Though the proposal bore some resemblance to the April 9 draft, it was much less favorable to the United States. By its terms Japan would agree to guarantee a "neutralized" Philippines, but the general pledge to refrain from the use of force in the Southwest Pacific was deleted. Also missing was the restriction on Japan's obligation under the Tripartite Pact. The new draft even called for the United States to cease assisting one European power against another. Other provisions, as in the April 9 draft, required the United States to lift its embargo measures, help Japan get products from Southeast Asia, and force China to conclude a settlement with Japan by withdrawing aid.

The American counterdraft which Hull gave to Nomura on May 16 revealed that the two governments were poles apart. This proposal reinserted the pledge to refrain from the use of force in the Southwest Pacific, restated the restriction on Japan's role under the Tripartite Pact, and projected a China settlement based upon respect for China's sovereignty. The only significant concession to the Japanese on the China question was a statement that the United States would negotiate over Manchuria, a hint that it might abandon its long-held policy of nonrecognition of Manchukuo.

Responding to Japanese Belligerence

While the talks went on at Washington, Japanese policy was suddenly thrown into a state of confusion by Hitler's attack on Russia. When Matsuoka visited Berlin in April, the Germans had given some hints that not all was well between Germany and Russia. But it was not until June 6 that Tokyo was given definite word that Russia would be

attacked. Despite that news, the Konoye government was intent upon pursuing the southward advance. On June 22, just a few hours before the Nazi attack on Russia, the cabinet decided to go forward with the plans to occupy southern Indochina. Such a move would obviously be in preparation for an attack on other areas of Southeast Asia. As soon as Matsuoka learned of the German attack, he excitedly urged that Japan also attack Russia. He insisted that Japan could strike in the north, then move south into Southeast Asia, and in the interim settle the China Incident! Matsuoka was not to get his way. On June 25 a liaison conference decided not to strike at Russia but to demand bases in southern French Indochina. At an imperial conference on July 2, the decision was ratified, and on July 12 the demand for bases was presented to Vichy France.

The decision of July 2 took into account the likelihood of war with Britain and the United States. The document which was adopted stated succinctly, "We will not be deterred by the possibility of being involved in a war with England and America." As early as July 12, Magic intercepts revealed to Washington the planned Japanese move into southern Indochina, but several weeks passed before they disclosed that part of the decision regarding possible war with the United States and Britain. Lieutenant Commander Alvin D. Kramer, who headed the navy unit that processed the intercepts, was finally able to piece the information together in early August. Included in the intercepts which Kramer sent to the State Department at that time was one stating that Japan would immediately begin to "arm for all out war against Britain and the United States to break the British-American encirclement."

Before the State Department received this ominous information, the Japanese had moved into southern Indochina, and the United States had reacted. On July 21, Vichy capitulated to the Japanese demands, agreeing that Japan could set up eight airfields and two naval bases and also maintain an unlimited number of troops in southern Indochina. Magic revealed that Japanese forces would move in on July 24. On July 23, Welles informed Nomura that the United States was breaking off the informal talks. The next day, as Japanese troops poured into southern Indochina, Roosevelt gave Nomura a stiff warning. If Japan attempted to seize the oil supplies of the Netherlands East Indies, said the president, the Dutch would resist, the British would assist them, "and in view of our own policy of assisting Great Britain, an exceedingly serious situation would immediately result." Roosevelt then proposed the neutralization of Indochina. On the

With Japan advancing deep into Indochina and arming for war against America, FDR froze Japanese assets in the United States. These Japanese rush to make inquiries at Seattle's Sumitomo bank.

Keystone

following day, July 25, he publicly announced that he was issuing an executive order freezing Japanese assets in the United States. This measure would bring all trade with Japan under government control.

Within the Roosevelt administration there was initial indecision about whether to cut the flow of oil to Japan under the freezing arrangement. Admiral Richmond Kelly Turner, head of the War Plans Division, and Admiral Stark, chief of naval operations, opposed an oil embargo on the grounds that it would cause Japan to attack the Netherlands East Indies. At first Roosevelt decided to let Japan have a limited amount of low grade petroleum. In the weeks that followed, however, no export licenses for oil were issued. Day by day, Japan's oil reserves fell lower and lower. Britain, the Dominions, and the Dutch joined in the oil embargo, and there was no way that Japan could replenish its dwindling oil stocks. Japan now had to pull back from its imperial objectives or plunge recklessly ahead. Japanese navy leaders were by no means anxious to plunge. On July 31, Admiral Osami Nagano, chief of the navy general staff, told the emperor that the navy wanted to avoid war with the United States if possible. Despite the worries of Japanese naval leaders, Japan's policy was not deflected. Matsuoka had been ousted from the government in a cabinet shuffle in mid-July, but the new foreign minister, Teijiro Toyoda, sent instructions to Nomura which revealed no softening of the Japanese position. On August 6, Nomura asked that the talks be reopened, and he presented a new draft agreement. The only significant change was the addition of a provision stating that Japan would not withdraw from Indochina until the China Incident was ended and Japan's "special position" in Indochina was recognized. Nomura also relayed a proposal from Premier Konoye for a personal meeting between himself and Roosevelt. To these proposals Hull made no immediate reply. Roosevelt was just then preparing to leave for the Atlantic Conference off the Newfoundland coast. Policy decisions would therefore have to await the outcome of the president's talks with Churchill.

The problem of Japan was given high priority during the talks. Churchill sought agreement on a joint warning to Japan that would involve the United States in a commitment to give armed aid in the Pacific. Roosevelt was unwilling to go that far, but he did agree to warn Japan unilaterally that in the event of an attack on British or Dutch possessions, the United States would take countermeasures, even though these measures "might result in war between the United States and Japan." Churchill thus got only limited support so far as formal diplomatic steps were concerned. He nevertheless came away from the conference much encouraged. When, later in August, Australia pressed Britain to obtain a firm commitment from the United States, the Australian government was informed that, although at the Atlantic meeting the United

States did not make any satisfactory declaration on the point, the general impression derived by Churchill was that "there was no doubt that in practice we could count on United States support if, as a result of Japanese aggression, we became involved in war with Japan."

When Roosevelt gave Nomura a warning on August 17, it was a slightly weaker one than had been agreed upon in the talks with Churchill. Hull had rephrased it to avoid the use of the word "war." The effect was further softened by Roosevelt's statement that the informal talks could be reopened in Washington. It now developed, however, that Japan was not interested in extended conversations. Nomura pressed insistently for a mid-Pacific meeting between Konoye and Roosevelt. In telegrams to Washington, Ambassador Grew strongly backed the project. Roosevelt expressed some interest in the proposal, but Hull was cool to the idea from the outset. Hull doubted that Konoye could agree to proposals that the United States could accept. In any case, he wanted to know before the meeting was held what might come out of it. It is now known from the Japanese records that Hull

Admiral Richmond Kelly Turner, head of the war plans division, advised Roosevelt not to cut off oil supplies to Japan. Such a step, he reasoned, would prompt Japan to attack the Netherlands East Indies.

was correct in his assessment of the matter. Though Japanese navy leaders endorsed the plan for a summit without qualification, the army leaders would not. Tojo, the war minister, told Konoye that if he met with Roosevelt, he must stick to the position already taken in the negotiations. Also, he must go to such a meeting with the firm determination, in case of failure, to return to Japan and lead the nation in war against the United States.

While the question of a Roosevelt-Konoye meeting was still undecided, Japanese army leaders pressed for an October deadline for a decision on peace or war. At a liaison conference on September 3, it was apparent that the army was going to get what it wanted. When the emperor learned of this at a meeting with Konoye and the army and navy chiefs, he was alarmed. During the course of General Hajime Sugiyama's explanation that the initial phase of the planned operations in Southeast Asia would take about three months, the emperor broke in abruptly and reminded Sugiyama that as war minister in 1937 he had asserted that the China Incident would be over in a month and it was still going on after four years. For this Sugiyama had no reply. When an imperial conference was held on September 6, the emperor's anxieties were again evident. At that meeting he read a peace poem written by his grandfather, the great Meiji emperor. He told the assembled leaders that his own efforts were directed at introducing in his own time the spirit of his grandfather's love for peace. The gathering was dumb-struck, and Navy Minister Koshiro Oikawa assured the emperor that diplomacy would be stressed. The conference nevertheless went on to agree that if by the early part of October there was no prospect of attaining Japan's demands, then they should "immediately decide to open hostilities against the United States, Great Britain, and the Netherlands."

The October deadline passed with no progress being made in the negotiations with the United States. On the contrary, on October 2 Hull informed Nomura that a conference between Konoye and Roosevelt would have to be postponed until there was a real meeting of minds. Konoye was now desperate. He knew that the United States would not agree to an overall settlement that allowed Japanese troops to remain in China, and he now pleaded with Tojo to agree to withdraw the troops. Tojo refused. If that were done, said the war minister, the sacrifices of more than four years would come to nought and Chinese contempt for Japan would grow. The loss of prestige that would accompany such a withdrawal at the command of the United States, he said, would have repercussions in Manchuria and Korea as well.

When Konoye reminded Tojo of a calculation indicating that Japan probably could not win a protracted war, Tojo declared that at some point during a man's lifetime, he might find it necessary to jump, with eyes closed, from the veranda of Kiyomizu temple. Since this Buddhist temple overlooked a high cliff, Konoye had no difficulty understanding the meaning of Tojo's words. He said to Tojo that such an idea might occur to an individual, but that as the premier of Japan, responsible for a 2,600-year-old national polity and a country of 100 million people, he could not adopt such an approach to the empire's problems.

There was no way out for the premier but to resign, and this he did on October 16. Konoye was content to see Tojo himself become premier if the October deadline could be set aside. The emperor intervened to assure that this would come about. When he named Tojo to the premiership, he commanded that the whole question of peace or war be restudied and that the new ministry not be bound by the decisions of the imperial conference of September 6. Konoye's hopes for a change in policy were nevertheless soon dashed. Tojo was convinced, as he later testified, that with dwindling oil reserves, the elasticity of Japan's national power was on the point of extinction. Furthermore, navy leaders were no longer willing to pit themselves against the army in the struggle over peace or war. The navy now adopted the position that it was up to the cabinet to decide that question; the navy would take orders.

The navy thus allowed Tojo to dominate the liaison conference held November 1–2, which drew up final proposals to be submitted to the United States. Two plans emerged from the meeting, later designated by American cryptologists as "Plan A" and "Plan B." The first listed Japan's terms for an overall settlement; the second was a stopgap proposal to be presented in the event that Plan A was rejected. A November 30 deadline for America's acceptance was also adopted. Tojo probably did not believe these decisions made war inevitable. To some extent he seemed to cling to Matsuoka's view that if Japan acted in a determined way, Washington might still yield.

The Final Impasse

After ratification by an imperial conference on November 5, the two plans were telegraphed to Nomura in Washington. The ambassador was given a November 25 deadline for wringing assent from the United States. On November 7 he presented Plan A to Hull. The draft did not list all the terms of a possible agreement; it focused on the few most disputed points. It called on the United States to compel Nationalist China to make peace by withdrawing aid. Japanese army units of unspecified size were to remain in certain areas of North China, Inner Mongolia, and Hainan for a "necessary period." Hull knew through Magic intercepts that Tokyo interpreted that to mean "about twenty-five years." Plan A would permit Japanese forces to remain in Indochina until the war in China was settled or a "just peace" was established in East Asia. As for the Tripartite Pact, Japan would be free to fulfill its obligations without restriction. Hull and Roosevelt pondered these terms for a week and then rejected them.

Shortly thereafter a special envoy, Saburo Kurusu, arrived to aid Nomura in the final negotiations. On November 20, Nomura and Kurusu presented Plan B to Hull. It demanded that the United States cut off aid to China, cancel its freezing order, supply Japan with a required quantity of oil, and help Japan get products from the Netherlands East Indies. In return for this, Japan would withdraw its troops from southern Indochina into northern Indochina and would join the United States in a pledge to make no armed advance in Southeast Asia and the South Pacific. While these terms were being considered, Hull learned through Magic that Nomura's deadline had been moved from November 25 to November 29. He also learned that the telegram from Tokyo extending the deadline said that after November 29 "things are automatically going to happen."

Hull and other American leaders fully realized that rejection of Plan B would almost certainly mean war in Southeast Asia. Still unknown, however, was whether American territory was included in the Japanese offensive plans. The general assumption was that Japan would likely avoid attacking the United States and that the Roosevelt administration would be faced with the alternative of entering the war on its own initiative or seeing Britain suffer defeat in Southeast Asia. There was agreement within the administration that such a defeat could not be permitted, not because the United States was interested in protecting British colonies, but because defeat in Southeast Asia would greatly impair Britain's war effort in Europe, both through loss of men and materiel and through loss of the tin, rubber, and other products of Southeast Asia. When Roosevelt polled his cabinet as to whether the American people would back the government if it struck at Japan in case it attacked English or Dutch territories in the Pacific, the entire cabinet agreed that the public would support the government. American military leaders, who were by no means anxious for war in the Pacific, concurred in the belief that the British and the Dutch could not be left to fight alone. On November 5 they recommended to Roosevelt that the United States go to war if Japan attacked British or Dutch territories or if Japan moved into Thailand west of 100° East or south of 10° North.

What leaders in Washington did not know was that Japan intended not only to attack American territory but also to destroy the fleet at Hawaii. In October, Admiral Yamamoto had finally convinced his fellow naval leaders to accept the Pearl Harbor attack plan. Shortly thereafter Tojo and the emperor were told of the plan. Many cabinet members, including the foreign minister, Shigenori Togo, were not told of it prior to the actual attack on December 8 (December 7, Washington time).

In Washington such a move by Japan was not expected. Intercepted messages revealed an important clue, but it was ignored. On September 24, Consul General Nagao Kita in Honolulu was instructed to divide Pearl Harbor into five subareas and to send detailed information on the movement of ships. When this instruction was intercepted, Colonel Rufus S. Bratton, chief of the army's G-2 Far Eastern Section, believed it to be of great significance, but his fellow officers thought it just another example of the Japanese obsession with detail. The intercept was not forwarded to top military and government leaders. Both civilian and military leaders in Washington were inclined to believe that if Japan did strike at American territory, the attack would come in areas far to the west of Hawaii. When Washington sent a warning to Pacific commanders on November 24, it warned of a possible surprise aggressive movement by Japan "in any direction including attack on Philippines or Guam."

As this warning went out, Hull drafted a counterproposal to Japan in the form of a three-month agreement. Hull's draft would require Japan not only to withdraw its forces from southern Indochina but also to limit its troops in northern Indochina to 25,000. Freezing restrictions would be removed, but the United States would still be permitted to keep export control measures in effect for reasons of national defense. Both powers would agree not to make any advance across any international border in the Pacific area. From what is now known from the Japanese records, there is little doubt that these terms would have been swiftly rejected if they had been presented. They were, however, never given to Japan because Hull failed to get support for them from Britain and China. The British believed the terms too favorable to Japan, and the Chinese feared that concessions to Japan would put a severe strain on their capacity to continue resistance to Japanese forces in China. Churchill dealt the scheme the *coup de grâce* when he telegraphed Roosevelt on the evening of November 25 reminding him that if China collapsed, "our joint dangers would enormously increase."

Instead of presenting the proposal to Japan, Hull gave Nomura on November 26 a Ten Point Program which essentially reaffirmed the position the United States had taken throughout the informal talks. Hull knew that the talking was now over. When Secretary of War Stimson inquired the next morning what had been done, Hull replied, "I have washed my hands of it and it is now in the hands of you and Knox—the Army and the Navy." That day, November 27, warnings went to commanders

Once the surprise air strike against Pearl Harbor
had been agreed, preparations went ahead speedily.
Right: Young Japanese pilots train on the eve
of Japan's entry into the war.

in the Pacific. The army warning said that hostile action by Japan was possible at any moment and that if hostilities could not be avoided, the United States desired that Japan commit the first overt act. The navy warning said, "This dispatch is to be considered a war warning." The text of the dispatch shows, however, that leaders in Washington still had their eyes more on Southeast Asia than Hawaii. The warning advised that Japanese troop concentrations indicated possible operations against the Philippines, Thailand, or Borneo.

Countdown to December 7

As war in the Pacific approached, British and Dominion leaders had one question uppermost in their minds: would the lead given by the United States in talking with Japan be followed by a similar lead in armed defense against Japan? The British believed the Japanese were poised to attack Thailand's Kra Isthmus just north of Malaya. While agonizing over whether to anticipate a Japanese move into the area, Churchill sent an urgent inquiry to Washington asking for a commitment of armed support. For many months the British had sought such a commitment. Now, on the eve of war, they got it. Roosevelt told the British ambassador, Lord Halifax, on December 1 that if Japan attacked the Dutch or the British, "we should obviously all be together." Two days later, Roosevelt told Halifax that when he talked of giving support to the British and the Dutch in the Far East, he meant "armed support." He said that he agreed with the British plan for operations in the Kra Isthmus if Japan attacked Thailand and that Britain could count on American support, though in this contingency support might not be forthcoming for a few days. Roosevelt's commitment to give armed support went beyond his constitutional authority. There is little doubt, however, that he intended to present the question of peace or war to Congress and that he expected Congress to immediately back the commitment.

In Japan, meanwhile, events raced toward war. An advance force of twenty-seven submarines left Japanese ports November 18–20 and headed for Hawaii, where they would take up patrol stations on December 5. On November 26, the main naval task force under the command of Admiral Chuichi Nagumo steamed out of Hitokappu Bay in the Kurile Islands and began its course to Hawaii. On December 1, an imperial conference made the final decision for war. The next day the date for the commencement of hostilities was set. An order was flashed to Admiral Nagumo: "Ascend Mt. Niitake! 1208." In clear text the message read: "Attack as planned! December 8." The same day instructions were sent to Japanese diplomatic and consular posts in

Hong Kong, Singapore, Batavia, Manila, Washington, and London to destroy most of their codes and ciphers. This message was intercepted and forwarded to the commander of the fleet at Pearl Harbor, Admiral Husband E. Kimmel, but he thought it meant only that Japan was about to invade Thailand.

The emperor's assent to the war decision was given with the clear injunction that a declaration of war precede the attack. This presented a problem to Japanese navy and army leaders because of the need for surprise, but they found Foreign Minister Togo very cooperative. He drafted a final note to the United States which concluded by saying only that it was "impossible to reach an agreement through further negotiation." Togo took the position that this was equivalent to a declaration of war. Then he agreed that the note should be delivered at 1:00 PM Washington time without even being told when or where the attack would take place. He was satisfied with the assurance given by the navy that this would leave a "sufficient margin of time." In fact this allowed a margin of only about thirty minutes. The slightest slip-up could thus result in the attack preceding the delivery of the note.

The final message to Washington was in fourteen parts, with notification of the ending of negotiations in the fourteenth. The first thirteen parts arrived in Washington in the afternoon and evening of December 6. The Japanese embassy deciphered the text by midnight. Meanwhile, the material had been intercepted by American units, and it went to the president that evening. That same night Roosevelt sent an appeal to the Japanese emperor, but since it offered no concessions, there could be little hope for a favorable reply. As it turned out, the message was held up over ten hours by the censorship office in Tokyo, and it reached the emperor too late to have any impact on events. Early in the morning of Sunday, December 7, the fourteenth part of the final Japanese note arrived in Washington, together with instructions to Nomura to deliver the entire note at 1:00 PM that day. Since Tokyo had sent strict instructions that only top-level personnel handle the message, the typing had to be done by a diplomatic secretary, whose typing skill proved inadequate. Amazingly, none of the first thirteen parts had been typed up in clean copy the preceding evening. The American deciphering effort was more efficient. The entire fourteen parts had been intercepted, deciphered, typed, and delivered to Hull and Roosevelt by midmorning December 7. At the Japanese embassy time was running out. As Nomura stood impatiently beside the struggling typist, mistakes multiplied. When it was apparent that the 1:00 PM delivery time could not be met, Nomura called the State Department and postponed his appointment to 1:45. When Nomura and Kurusu reached the department at about 2:00 PM, the bombs had already been falling on Pearl Harbor for more than thirty minutes. Hull knew of the attack and accorded the Japanese a chilly interview.

In the final hours, as the clasp of war was closing, many signs had pointed to a surprise attack on Pearl Harbor, but all were either overlooked or misinterpreted. At Hawaii, a Japanese navy ensign, Takeo Yoshikawa, disguised as Vice Consul Morimura, received instructions to send daily reports on ship locations and information on whether the fleet was protected by torpedo nets and balloons. This telegram was intercepted and deciphered but not translated. On December 6, a translator in the Navy Cryptographic Section in Washington glanced at the intercept but did not translate it. At Pearl Harbor, elements of the Japanese advanced submarine force were spotted well before the attack. At 3:55 AM, December 7, the United States Navy minesweeper *Condor* sighted a submarine off the entrance to the harbor, and at 6:45 the destroyer *Ward* dropped depth charges on a submarine. Reports of these contacts were treated at Pearl Harbor as unconfirmed reports or mistaken drill messages. At 7:02

AM a radar unit of the Army Aircraft Warning Service (AWS) spotted the Japanese attack planes 137 miles north of Pearl Harbor. The officer in charge of the AWS Information Center assumed that it was a flight of B-17s which was due to arrive from the mainland that morning, and he did nothing. If the report had been correctly interpreted, Pearl Harbor would have had over fifty minutes' warning before the Japanese attacked.

The attack on Pearl Harbor, delivered without a declaration of war, aroused great indignation among the American people. Roosevelt expressed the feelings of his fellow Americans when he called December 7, 1941, "a date which will live in infamy." The success of the attack also led to bitter controversy over the assessment of blame on the American side. Some critics charged that Roosevelt deliberately exposed the fleet at Pearl Harbor so as to lure the Japanese into an attack which would arouse the nation behind him. A notation by Stimson in his diary after a cabinet meeting on November 25 lends support to this theory: "The question was how we should maneuver them into firing the first shot without allowing too much danger to ourselves." It was also charged that intercepts were deliberately withheld from the American comman-

Zeros prepare to take off from an aircraft carrier in this painting by Shuri Arai, a Japanese artist. Until 1943, the Zero was superior in performance to the American fighters.

ders in Hawaii in order to ensure the success of the Japanese attack.

The great bulk of evidence now available, however, argues conclusively against such a conspiracy theory. Stimson's comments were a reflection of his own belligerent inclinations and careless writing rather than an accurate indication of Roosevelt's policy. Stimson must have known that no one was "maneuvering" the Japanese in 1941. It is true that much of the information gleaned from intercepts was not sent to Hawaii, but this resulted from concern over the security of the deciphering operation and from sheer negligence. Both Admiral Stark and General Sherman Miles, head of army intelligence, mistakenly believed that the navy had at Hawaii both a machine capable of deciphering the top-secret Japanese codes and a cryptographic unit processing intercepts. Roosevelt was certainly not withholding intercepts from Hawaii. He had great difficulty getting them himself, and he never did get the actual texts of them until November 1941, when he flatly asserted his presidential authority and demanded them. Even then he did not get important items. The intercept revealing the 1:00 PM delivery time for the final Japanese note was only given orally to his aide. It did not reach the president. He also did not get earlier intercepts which revealed a possible threat to Hawaii. In retrospect, it is apparent that the telegraphic traffic between Tokyo and the Japanese consulate general in Hawaii was the most significant, and this was given a low priority. Many of those telegrams were not processed until after December 7, and those which were processed in time were not sent to Roosevelt. The information that did reach the president was misleading. When in late November he questioned Admiral Stark about Pearl Harbor, he was told that the base was in no danger and that the fleet was at sea.

Right up to the last, American leaders had their eyes on the Philippines rather than Hawaii. When General Marshall, the army chief, sent a warning on the morning of December 7, General Leonard T. Gerow, head of the War Plans Division, told the officer handling the warning, "If there's any question of priority, give it first to the Philippines." When the attack on Pearl Harbor came, the surprise in Washington was genuine. The broadcast from Hawaii said tersely: "Air raid Pearl Harbor—this is no drill." When this was handed to the secretary of the navy, Frank Knox, he exclaimed: "My God, this can't be true! This must mean the Philippines!" "No, sir," said Admiral Stark, "This is Pearl!"

The fervor of the Japanese martial spirit is captured in this oil by M. Susuki showing pilots after graduation. When the fleet set course for Pearl Harbor in November 1941, the sailors and naval airmen believed their nation's destiny would soon be fulfilled.

Bibliography

GENERAL

*Adler, Selig, *The Uncertain Giant, 1921–1941: American Foreign Policy between the Wars* (New York, 1965)

*Carr, E. H., *The Twenty Years' Crisis, 1919–1939: An Introduction to the Study of International Relations* (New York, 1939)

*Chatfield, Charles, *For Peace and Justice: Pacifism in America, 1914–1941* (Knoxville, Tenn., 1971)

Ferrell, Robert H., "The Price of Isolation: American Diplomacy, 1921–1945," in Leuchtenburg, William E., ed., *The Unfinished Century* (Boston, 1973)

Gathorne-Hardy, G. M., *A Short History of International Affairs, 1920–39* (4th edn., London, 1950)

Nelson, John K., *The Peace Prophets: American Pacifist Thought, 1919–1941* (Chapel Hill, N.C., 1967)

Nevins, Allan, *The New Deal in World Affairs* (New Haven, 1950)

Nevins, Allan, *The United States in a Chaotic World, 1918–1933* (New Haven, 1950)

*Osgood, Robert E., *Ideals and Self-Interest in American Foreign Relations* (Chicago, 1953)

Smith, Robert Freeman. "American Foreign Relations, 1920–1942," in Bernstein, Barton J., ed., *Towards a New Past: Dissenting Essays in American History* (New York, 1968)

Chapter 1: THE COLLAPSE OF WORLD ORDER

Ashby, Leroy, *The Spearless Leader: Senator Borah and the Progressive Movement in the 1920's* (Urbana, Ill., 1972)

Brandes, Joseph, *Herbert Hoover and Economic Diplomacy: Department of Commerce Policy, 1921–1928* (Pittsburgh, 1962)

Buckley, Thomas H., *The United States and the Washington Conference, 1921–1922* (Knoxville, Tenn., 1970)

Ellis, L. Ethan, *Frank B. Kellogg and American Foreign Relations, 1925–1929* (New Brunswick, N.J., 1961)

Ellis, Lewis Ethan, *Republican Foreign Policy, 1921–1933* (New Brunswick, N.J., 1968)

*Ferrell, Robert H., *American Diplomacy in the Great Depression: Hoover-Stimson Foreign Policy, 1929–1933* (New Haven, 1957)

Ferrell, Robert H., *Peace in their Time: The Origins of the Kellogg-Briand Pact* (New Haven, 1952)

Fleming, Denna F., *The United States and World Organization, 1920–1933* (New York, 1938)

Glad, Betty, *Charles Evans Hughes and the Illusions of Innocence: A Study in American Diplomacy* (Urbana, Ill., 1966)

O'Connor, Raymond G., *Perilous Equilibrium: The United States and the London Naval Conference of 1930* (Lawrence, Kans., 1962)

Roskill, Stephen, *Naval Policy Between the Wars. Vol. 1: The Period of Anglo-American Antagonism, 1919–1929* (New York, 1968)

Stoner, John E. S., *S. O. Levinson and the Pact of Paris* (Chicago, 1943)

Williams, William A., "The Legend of Isolationism in the 1920's," *Science and Society*, XVIII (1954)

Wilson, Joan Hoff, *American Business and Foreign Policy, 1920–1933* (Lexington, Ky., 1971)

Chapter 2: TOWARD UNITY IN THE HEMISPHERE

*Cline, Howard F., *The United States and Mexico* (rev. edn., Cambridge, Mass., 1963)

Cronon, E. David, *Josephus Daniels in Mexico* (Madison, Wis., 1960)

de Conde, Alexander, *Herbert Hoover's Latin American Policy* (Stanford, Cal., 1951)

Dozer, Donald M., *Are We Good Neighbors? Three Decades of Inter-American Relations* (Gainesville, Fla., 1959)

Green, David, *The Containment of Latin America: A History of the Myths and Realities of the Good Neighbor Policy* (Chicago, 1971)

Guerrant, Edward O., *Roosevelt's Good Neighbor Policy* (Albuquerque, N.M., 1950)

Kanman, William, *A Search for Stability: United States Diplomacy Toward Nicaragua, 1925–1933* (Notre Dame, Ind., 1968)

Smith, Robert Freeman, *The United States and Revolutionary Nationalism in Mexico, 1916–1932* (Chicago, 1972)

*Wood, Bryce, *The Making of the Good Neighbor Policy* (New York, 1961)

Wood, Bryce, *The United States and Latin-American Wars, 1932–1942* (New York, 1966)

Chapter 3: FIREBELL IN THE EAST

Borg, Dorothy, *The United States and the Far Eastern Crisis of 1933–1938* (Cambridge, Mass., 1964)

Borg, Dorothy, & Okamoto, Shumpei, eds., *Pearl Harbor as History: Japanese-American Relations, 1931–1941* (New York, 1973)

Buhite, Russell D., *Nelson T. Johnson and American Policy Toward China, 1925–1941* (East Lansing, Mich., 1968)

Griswold, Alfred W., *The Far Eastern Policy of the United States* (New York, 1938)

*Morison, Elting E., *Turmoil and Tradition: A Study of the Life and Times of Henry L. Stimson* (Boston, 1960)

Perry, Hamilton D., *The Panay Incident: Prelude to Pearl Harbor* (New York, 1969)

Rappaport, Armin L., *Henry L. Stimson and Japan, 1931–1933* (Chicago, 1963)

Varg, Paul A., *The Closing of the Door: Sino-American Relations, 1936–1946* (East Lansing, Mich., 1973)

Wheeler, Gerald E., *Prelude to Pearl Harbor: The United States Navy and the Far East, 1921–1931* (Columbia, Mo., 1963)

Chapter 4: THE FASCIST THREAT

Cole, Wayne S., *Senator Gerald P. Nye and American Foreign Relations* (Minneapolis, 1962)

*Divine, Robert A., *The Illusion of Neutrality* (Chicago, 1962)

Feis, Herbert, *1933: Characters in Crisis* (Boston, 1966)

*Gardner, Lloyd C., *Economic Aspects of New Deal Diplomacy* (Madison, Wis., 1964)

Guttmann, Allen, *Wound in the Heart: America and the Spanish Civil War* (New York, 1962)

Harris, Brice, Jr., *The United States and the Italo-Ethiopian Crisis* (Stanford, Cal., 1964)

Israel, Fred L., *Nevada's Key Pittman* (Lincoln, Neb., 1963)

*Jonas, Manfred, *Isolationism in America, 1935–1941* (Ithaca, 1966)

McKenna, Marian C., *Borah* (Ann Arbor, Mich., 1961)

Offner, Arnold A., *American Appeasement: United States Foreign Policy and Germany, 1933–1938* (Cambridge, Mass., 1968)

Pratt, Julius W., *Cordell Hull, 1933–44* (New York, 1964)

Wiltz, John E., *In Search of Peace: The Senate Munitions Inquiry, 1934–1936* (Baton Rouge, 1963)

Chapter 5: AN END TO NEUTRALITY

Chadwin, Mark L., *The Hawks of World War II: The Interventionist Movement in the United States Prior to Pearl Harbor* (Chapel Hill, N.C., 1968)

Cole, Wayne S., *America First: The Battle Against Intervention, 1940–1941* (Madison, Wis., 1953)

Compton, James V., *The Swastika and the Eagle: Hitler, the United States, and the origins of World War II* (Boston, 1967)

Dawson, Raymond H., *The Decision to Aid Russia, 1941: Foreign and Domestic Politics* (Chapel Hill, N.C., 1959)

*Divine, Robert A., *Reluctant Belligerent: American Entry into the Second World War* (New York, 1965)

Drummond, Dwight F., *The Passing of American Neutrality, 1937–1941* (Ann Arbor, Mich., 1955)

Fehrenbach, T. R., *F.D.R.'s Undeclared War, 1939 to 1941* (New York, 1967)

Friedlander, Saul, *Prelude to Downfall: Hitler and the United States, 1939–1941* (New York, 1967)

Friedman, Donald J., *The Road from Isolation: The Campaign of the American Committee for Non-Participation in Japanese Aggression, 1938–1941* (Cambridge, Mass., 1968)

Haight, John M., Jr., *American Aid to France, 1938–1940* (New York, 1970)

Kimball, Warren F., *The Most Unsordid Act: Lend-Lease, 1939–1941* (Baltimore, 1969)

*Langer, William L., & Gleason, S. Everett, *The Challenge to Isolation, 1937–1940* (New York, 1952)

*Langer, William L., & Gleason, S. Everett, *The Undeclared War, 1940–1941* (New York, 1953)

*indicates paperback

Lu, David J., *From the Marco Polo Bridge to Pearl Harbor: Japan's Entry into World War II* (Washington, D.C., 1961)

Rauch, Basil, *Roosevelt: From Munich to Pearl Harbor* (New York, 1950)

Schwartz, Andrew J., *America and the Russo-Finnish War* (Washington, D.C., 1960)

Trefousse, Hans L., *Germany and American Neutrality, 1939–1941* (New York, 1951)

Wilson, Theodore A., *The First Summit: Roosevelt and Churchill at Placentia Bay, 1941* (Boston, 1969)

Chapter 6: A DAY OF INFAMY

Adams, Frederick C., "The Road to Pearl Harbor: A Reexamination of American Far Eastern Policy, July 1937–December 1938," *Journal of American History*, LVIII (1971)

Baker, Leonard, *Roosevelt and Pearl Harbor: A Great President in Time of Crisis* (New York, 1970)

Beard, Charles A., *President Roosevelt and the Coming of the War, 1941* (New Haven, 1948)

Butow, Robert J., *Tojo and the Coming of the War* (Princeton, 1961)

Conroy, Hilary, "The Strange Diplomacy of Admiral Nomura," *Proceedings of the American Philosophical Society*, CXIV (1970)

*Feis, Herbert, *The Road to Pearl Harbor* (Princeton, 1950)

Ike, Nobutaka, trans. and ed., *Japan's Decision for War: Records of the 1941 Policy Conferences* (Stanford, Cal., 1968)

Millis, Walter, *This is Pearl! The United States and Japan—1941* (New York, 1947)

Potter, John Dean, *Yamamoto: The Man who Menaced America* (New York, 1965)

Schroeder, Paul W., *The Axis Alliance and Japanese-American Relations, 1941* (Ithaca, N.Y., 1958)

Tansill, Charles C., *Back Door to War: The Roosevelt Foreign Policy, 1933–1941* (Chicago, 1952)

*Wohlstetter, Roberta, *Pearl Harbor: Warning and Decision* (Stanford, Cal., 1962)

Disaster, which threatened the Allies on every front when the United States was pitchforked into war on December 7, 1941, was in fact to be narrowly averted. But many dark days lay ahead for them, and not for some time after Pearl Harbor did the tide begin to turn. Ultimately, victory would be complete, but it would require an unparalleled national effort from the American people.

The Second World War would be a truly global struggle, as the First World War had not been. To defeat the Axis the United States would have to conduct—indeed, take the lead in —large-scale military and naval operations in two huge and widely separated theaters, both of them thousands of miles from home. She would have to mobilize 15 million men, perform miracles of industrial production, and spend sums roughly twice as large as the entire federal expenditure since 1789.

With the expansion of the armed forces and of the wartime economy, the problem of unemployment, which had defeated the New Deal, would at last be solved. The conflict would also have profound social consequences, uprooting millions, increasing marriage, birth, and divorce rates, and stimulating both education and religion. Yet the most momentous change would come in the attitudes of the American people to the outside world. The Second World War, by destroying the illusion that the United States could find security in isolation, would persuade nearly all Americans that they could no longer avoid the role of world leadership. Volume 16 relates the United States role in the war.